WORCESTER NUNNERIES

The Nuns of the Medieval Diocese

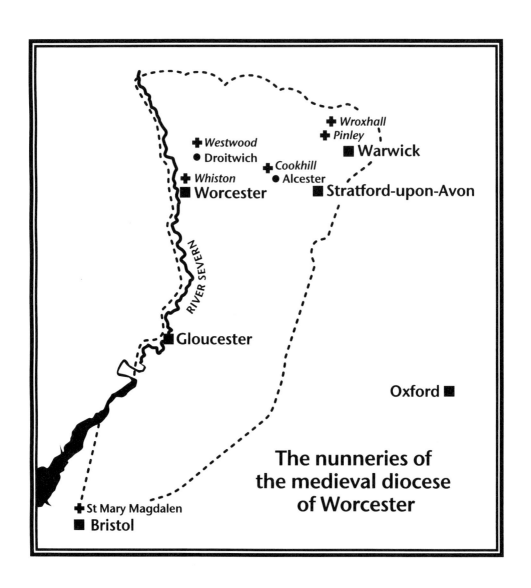

✚ Wroxhall
✚ Pinley
■ Warwick

✚ Westwood
● Droitwich
✚ Cookhill
✚ Whiston
● Alcester
■ Worcester
■ Stratford-upon-Avon

RIVER SEVERN

■ Gloucester

Oxford ■

The nunneries of
the medieval diocese
of Worcester

✚ St Mary Magdalen
■ Bristol

WORCESTER NUNNERIES

The Nuns of the Medieval Diocese

MARGARET GOODRICH

PHILLIMORE

2008

Published by
PHILLIMORE & CO. LTD
Chichester, West Sussex, England
www.phillimore.co.uk
www.thehistorypress.co.uk

ISBN 978-1-86077-591-8

Printed and bound in Great Britain

Contents

List of Illustrations

In memory of
Philip
and for my
daughters

Foreword

I first became fascinated by the local women religious when I realised that the Worcester school in which I was teaching stood beside the site of a medieval nunnery. My research sprang from there and soon included all the nunneries of the medieval Worcester diocese.

I have met many kind and interesting people along the way and value the new friendships made. My first thanks must go to Dr Joan Greatrex and Professor Donald Logan, both distinguished scholars, who have unstintingly given me advice and encouragement. At Worcester, Robin Whittaker and his staff at the Record Offices have been unfailingly patient and helpful, and at the Cathedral Library the late Canon Iain McKenzie, Dr David Morrison and Ron Stratton have always welcomed me and found the books and documents I needed. I have had similar care and interest from the staff of Hereford Cathedral Library and in my contacts with Warwick and Bristol Record Offices and the Central Library and the Museum and Art Gallery in Birmingham. Christopher Guy and David Kenrick have provided me with excellent photographs and Johnnie Pakington with a remarkable image of his 16th-century ancestor and namesake, Sir John Pakington. Finally my thanks go to Laurie King, indefatigable IT specialist. He has helped me in so many ways to prepare my text and illustrations for publication. For all these people and their work I am ever grateful.

This book is in many ways only an introduction to the life of Worcester's medieval nunneries. There is more that could be written but I hope that it will help to bring this group of women out of the shadows. Their story is a part of women's history as well as part of the religious, social and economic history of the medieval world.

I

Holy Women of Worcestershire

In the medieval world the Church was interwoven with all aspects of life. The religious orders were one of the integral parts of the Church; monks and nuns, and later friars, were to be found throughout Christendom. Their monastic buildings were part of the townscape and countryside, they held widespread land and property and their religious, social and economic influence was everywhere. Of the religious, the women, the nuns, were the least numerous and also the least visible since their enclosure rules were more enforceable than those for men. For example, monks who were also priests might ride out regularly to nearby churches belonging to the monastery to celebrate mass and the powerful abbots and priors often attended on the king or conferred with magnates, not only valued for their wisdom but also as important landholders in their own right.

In the Anglo-Saxon age, great abbesses such as Hilda of Whitby were the confidantes of kings and this role continued in the later medieval period. Kings and queens enjoyed monastic hospitality, bringing prestige to the monks or nuns they visited but also great expense. Among women's houses the Plantagenets loved the French abbey at Fontevrault; Henry II, his queen Eleanor of Aquitaine and their son, Richard the Lionheart, are all buried there. In England, Romsey Abbey and Amesbury were favourites with the royal family and Wilton was another female house that enjoyed royal visits. But the nunneries of medieval Worcestershire were not in this league. They were small modest houses, usually financially stretched, often indeed in poverty, with the nuns having to live the simplest life.

The medieval diocese of Worcester was far larger than the county of today. It spread southwards as far as north Bristol, covering most of today's Gloucestershire, as well as much of Warwickshire, including the towns of Warwick and Stratford-upon-Avon. While a number of nunneries lay within this widespread diocese, they were mostly congregated in the north, in Worcestershire and Warwickshire. Surprisingly, in post-Conquest times the Augustinian canonesses at Bristol were the only female house in Worcester diocese's extensive lands in Gloucestershire. Of the women's houses in Worcestershire, the best known today is the White Ladies of Worcester, also called Whiston Priory, which was situated half a mile to the north, beyond the city's Foregate. About five miles away was the nunnery at Westwood outside Droitwich and further still from Worcester was Cookhill Priory beyond Inkberrow, almost on the Warwickshire border. Within Warwickshire, not far west of Warwick, lay the priory of Wroxall and a smaller house at Pinley, only a short distance from each other. The house of St Mary Magdalene at Bristol was the most distant from Worcester; it appears as a small impoverished community and its records are sparse, yet it can still provide some useful information for this study.

Apart from the White Ladies, which was a 13th-century foundation, all the other houses date from a century earlier, but these 12th-century nuns were not the first communities of religious women in Worcestershire. Some fragmentary traces of earlier groups still remain. As early as the late seventh century there is mention of an abbess Cutsuida at Penitanham[1] which is probably Inkberrow in Worcestershire. More substantially, several eighth-century charters survive for the abbesses of Withington in Gloucestershire[2] and, of course, there was the nuns' house at Gloucester, later replaced by secular canons and then Benedictine monks in what eventually became the cathedral precinct. Almost certainly all these communities were small, grouped around an abbess of some social standing – Cutsuida may have been a Mercian princess – and they would have been double houses with men attached to support the women. The custom of men and women sharing a religious settlement was not new, even at this time. It had been one of the several forms of religious life that characterised Celtic Christianity and the tradition continued in such renowned Anglo-Saxon foundations as the Whitby of St Hilda and Etheldreda's Ely. On a smaller scale, the earliest Worcester female monasteries would have followed the same pattern and from the late eighth century would have sadly shared the same fate, disappearing in the violent chaos of Viking raid and invasion. The 10th-century revival, however, led by the inspiration of Archbishop Dunstan, Aethelwold of Winchester and Oswald of Worcester, established monastic life once again; it took root and flourished and women, though not as visible as men, undoubtedly returned to the religious life, some as anchoresses and hermits, others living in small groups often near a male house. At the great abbey of Evesham, five nuns are recorded among the men in 1086, where they may well have worked in the almonry helping the monks tend the poor, particularly the female poor, but they are not mentioned again in the monastic record.[3] A little earlier there is a hint of another group of holy women in Worcester City, including the saintly Bishop Wulstan's mother. In his book *The Life of St Wulstan* (Bishop of Worcester 1062-95), William of Malmesbury writes that when the boy Wulstan had grown up:

The young Wulstan's father and mother had both grown weary of the world and began to long and sigh earnestly for another habit and another way of life. Indeed old age and poverty lay before them. In no long time they satisfied their desire and his father took the monk's habit at Worcester, his mother the nun's veil in the same city.[4]

Thus his parents, with their gifted son and presumably any other children off their hands, could retire with clear consciences. Recruits to religious orders were not all young and many, like Wulstan's parents, joined for the last years of their lives. For widows, in particular, a women's convent provided safety, a certain comfort, and like-minded company. For wealthy widows it provided a sanctuary from predatory fortune hunters. Wulstan's mother's religious home may possibly have been outside the city wall at Whistones, where Sally Thompson suggests there was an intermittent female community, or more likely the holy women lived close to the cathedral priory; here the veil and the male community would give them protection and from a secluded position they might take a passive part in the daily services of the monastic church. Certainly this was the situation at Bec in Anselm's time when two women, Basilia, widow of Gerard de Gournay and Eva, widow of William Crispin, lived beside the abbey. Anselm welcomed them as his 'dearest mothers'. Similarly at another Norman monastery, St Evroult, two sisters, Judith and Emma Grandmesnil, found shelter when their family was disgraced. However, when they later wished to marry, they denied that they had ever taken the veil to become part of the community, although some still maintained that the abbot had bestowed it on them.

It appears then that in the 11th century women like these were to be found living singly or in small groups beside male Benedictine houses, but in the next century they seem to disappear, probably because of the unprecedented surge of new female houses. Amazingly, all over England more than 100 new foundations for women sprang up between 1130 and the end of the century. Most were houses of Benedictine nuns but some followed the Cistercian Rule and others were Augustinian canonesses. Exceptionally, a few of these new foundations provided for both men and women, although the old concept of men and women religious sharing a monastic life was largely abandoned in the great 12th-century revival.

But it was not entirely forgotten. In the centuries after the Conquest it became institutionalised by a handful of orders, among them the English Gilbertines, the order of Fontevrault and later the Bridgettines. In these orders careful provision was made for the two sexes to exist within one monastic enclosure, living separately, following the old Anglo-Saxon pattern. There were also less-formalised arrangements in many female Benedictine houses, with mentions of a prior or a master, a guardian or a custos or brothers appearing in the records of women's houses.

Nuns living in community were not the only women to take up the religious call. In the diocese of Worcester, as elsewhere, there were a number of women following other paths to the holy life. Some of these, permanently vowed to religion, lived as anchoresses. An anchoress usually occupied a 'cell', a small enclosure of one or two rooms beside a church in a town or city. Julian of Norwich is probably the best known but there were many others. At Bristol in 1503 the Hockaday Transcripts record that Dame Mawde Baker left the 'lady ancress at the blake Friars of Brystow 20s to be payable wekely 2d or more yf need be'.[5] In Worcester one Juliana seems to have been a long-term fixture beside St Nicholas Church, in the city's High Street. She was resident in 1256 when she was allowed 'to widen her court on the street to the north of the said church extending from the great high road to the wall of the city'[6] and she was still there eight years later when the king, Henry III, granted her two oaks from Feckenham Forest – were these for further building extensions?[7] Two years after that she gained a rent charge of 31s. a year on lands outside the city,[8] money presumably used for food and lights and to pay a servant to shop and cook for her and do the other small domestic tasks of the minute household. Unfortunately for modern historians, no visible trace of Juliana's accommodation remains. Eighteenth-century rebuilding swept away old medieval St Nicholas, so only an archaeological excavation might provide any trace of her anchorhold.

Although Juliana's life was physically extremely circumscribed, in other ways she was not isolated from the world. She might be called an 'inclusa', an enclosed one, yet she was less withdrawn than many a cloistered nun. Her enclosure would not prevent her from talking through her window with those who stopped to greet her or came to seek advice. Her immuring might have begun with a sombre, formal ceremony presided over by the bishop. In an anchoress' service surviving from the late 12th century at Canterbury, after Mass had been celebrated with special scripture readings, the recluse passed into her cell, her 'sepulcher', the bishop having already sprinkled it with holy water and incense, singing, 'Here I will stay for ever; this is the home I have chosen.' More prayers were said, those used for the dead at burial, for the recluse in theory had left the world;[9] she was now sealed up as in her coffin, although, in fact, she continued, very much alive. Some recluses, like Julian of Norwich, led most holy lives and were deep sources of prayer and spiritual guidance; others, according to Aelred of Rievaulx, were too taken up with gossip, leaning from their window chatting to friends interspersed with teaching children, or sorting out their small finances, to be of much spiritual light.

We cannot estimate what influence anchoresses had in Worcester but they continued until the Reformation. As late as 1521 an 'ankras' still dwelt in the city. Prior William More, the penultimate prior of the cathedral priory, 'payd for brycke lyme and sonde to ye reparacon' of her house 'by ye charnel hows,' presumably that on the north side of the cathedral church.[10] Ten years later in 1531 his register recorded further expenses – 20d. and 12d. – for rewards to 'ye Ancres'[11] and there is a last, sadder record of another anchoress during the dissolution of the monasteries in a description of when Richard Ingworth, Bishop of Dover, visited Worcester in 1538. Under Thomas Cromwell's command he was journeying through the realm suppressing or receiving the surrender of the friaries as he went. Despite having once been a senior Dominican friar he had little sympathy for the friars or for the 'ancress' he found in the Black Friars churchyard. Ingworth noted that he 'had not a lityll besynes to have her grauntt to cum owte, but owte sche is'.[12]

Obviously the anchoress tradition in the city was strong and continuous, but even determined devout women had to give way before the king's commissioners. Their veils, habits and their enclosed anchorholds would have smacked of the old order. They appeared too much like nuns and must go the same way. Another group of devotees to the religious life would have been more invisible and thus less vulnerable than the 'inclusae'. These were women who may have remained based in their own homes but lived under a religious rule of life. Sometimes a friend or relative, often a widow, joined them. They took vows of chastity and were devoted to prayer and good works, with the household organised to support them. The volatile and eccentric Margery Kempe of Lynn must be the best known of this type of woman. After years of married life and 13 children, she took a vow of chastity and set out, literally, to find a deeper spiritual life. Her journeyings took her here and there in England and to Rome and Compostella as well. More locally we find Isabele de Stepelton who, like Margery in intent but probably less extreme, in 1337 solemnly vowed to Bishop Thomas Hemenhale of Worcester:

> a dieux et a notre dame seynt Marie et a touz les seintz du ciel qe ieo diesores
> en chaste vie a servir dieux nettement en chastete.[13]

To pinpoint the history of such women (Margery Kempe is the exception) is not easy, as their rule of life was in one sense informal as they belonged to no official religious order. Their only formal act was their going to the bishop or his deputy, to make a life-changing private vow. Bishop Bransford's register records another devout woman, Alice Maidegod of Stow. In April 1347, the bishop's commissioners met her and:

> By means of an expert and discreet enquiry they examined the reasons why
> Alice Maidegod of Stow, widow, wished to take the vow of Chastity. Having
> found them to be sincere and appropriate, they bestowed benediction on
> Alice in accordance with their commission.[14]

Undoubtedly in Worcestershire, as elsewhere, there were several of these religious women who followed their vocation within their existing domestic situation, as evidence found mainly in the bishops' registers shows. These records also display interchange between the different groups of religious women. As their personal circumstances or spiritual development altered, women might move from one religious lifestyle to another. Sometimes a widow like Alice Maidegod might take a further step from the world and join a nunnery, or a nun feeling a call to seclusion might leave her sisters to become an anchoress or a hermit. Another pattern was when a group of lay sisters living together, all under the same vow of chastity and prayer, might take on the full regular religious life to become a community of nuns; there is evidence of this transition in Worcester.

Yet, although there were alternatives, for most women the call to the religious life was a call to the nunnery. Where should this be situated? Traditionally, since the days of the early Church, monasteries should be in the desert. This was literally true for the first monks in Egypt and even in the 12th century some still sought equivalent harsh, inhospitable 'desert' places. Here they believed Satan dwelt; here on the front line, armed with their prayers and sacrificial lives, the monks could wage war on the devil, protect and defend Christendom and keep evil at bay. Thus the Cistercians went to the barren moorland of Yorkshire or the wild borders of Wales, and the Praemonstratensians to the Lincolnshire coastal marsh. But these were no places for women, who usually became more safely established in or near a town or on a well-placed manor. Here the convent became the home where holy women followed their vocation. They lived in community and, ideally, the daily structure of repeated worship, the horarium, work, silence and the company of others helped them to fulfil their vows. Nuns also became fulfilled in another sense: to rise up the monastic ladder was almost the only career open to a single woman at this time. To hold office successfully in a religious community, however small, developed organisational and social skills only open in the lay world to wives of landowners left in charge of estates and households. For a single woman, the security and responsibilities of the cloistered community could offer a satisfying life's career.

This study of the nunneries of the later medieval Worcester diocese provides insight into the lives of the nuns, their family origins, their problems, their relationships with the world beyond their walls and the traumatic finale of the Dissolution. But first we turn to the founding of the nunneries themselves.

II

Founding

The late 11th century saw a great reform and reinvigoration of the Church, led by a dynamic and determined pope, the former monk, Hildebrand, now Gregory VII. His revitalising of western Christendom encouraged a surge of monastic zeal that lasted for more than a hundred years, bringing with it a flood of new foundations including many houses for women. Lay people as much as the clergy were enthused with renewed inspiration and between 1130 and 1200 at least 40 of the new houses for women in Southern England were lay foundations. Westwood and Cookhill, Wroxall and Pinley as well as the priory at Bristol, all founded in the mid-12th century, were all part of this religious flowering. Whiston alone came later, almost as an afterthought of the 13th century. By the late 1250s, when the Normans were securely settled in England and Henry II had restored civil peace, religious observance could move forward, already stimulated by the reforms of Pope Gregory VII and his contemporaries.

Westwood

A lay woman of noble family, Eustachia de Say, and her son, Osbert FitzHugh, first established Westwood Priory. The de Says were of the new French landowning aristocracy who had left Normandy for England nearly a hundred years before. Eustachia's husband's ancestor Richard Scrope, had crossed the Channel to settle in Herefordshire on land granted to him in Edward the Confessor's time when the Normans were already building up a powerful influence at court. No doubt Emma, Edward's Norman queen, encouraged this migration. Richard Scrope's grandson, Hugh FitzOsbern, Eustachia's husband, though no great aristocrat was a wealthy tenant-in-chief of the king and held substantial estates spread over the Midland shires. It seems that he had died by the 1150s, so it was his widow and son who provided for the new nunnery. Their founding grants included the site at Westwood outside medieval Wych, today's Droitwich, further land at Westwood as well as at neighbouring Crutch, a salt pit in Wych and the church and its dues at more distant Cotheridge. This was not an overwhelming endowment but fortunately Eustachia and her family had good connections whom they must have persuaded to join them in their enterprise. One was Ralph, Earl of Chester, another was Gundreda, Countess of Warwick, daughter of William de Warenne, Earl of Surrey, both greater and grander than the de Says. Ralph and Gundreda were both powerful magnates; she through her mother claimed direct descent from the great Emperor Charlemagne; they were supporters of the heir to the throne, Prince Henry, and keen to benefit from the peace that the young Plantagenet would bring after the devastating civil war of Stephen and Matilda. Locally, others of the landed and knightly class supported the new nunnery. Richard de Portes of Elmley gave it land and a mill at Droitwich, William de Poer, the under-sheriff, donated a chapel at Pirton and tithes at Guiting in Gloucestershire; land at Bromfield in Shropshire came from Ingelard of Stretton. Berenice Kerr[1] points out that many of these people were of the Angevin party, supporters of Henry, heir apparent, who had shrewdly noted where Henry of Anjou's religious interests lay.

The Earl of Chester's involvement with the nunnery gives a strong pointer to the date of Westwood's founding. We know that he died in 1153; thus his gift to the priory of 40s. a year must have predated this.[2] Later in the decade, probably in April 1158, Henry, now king, confirmed the founding charter, which is long since lost, and Bishop Alfred of Worcester, briefly in office 1158-60, approved another grant to the nuns.[3] All this evidence indicates a house well established by 1160, and first set up before 1153.

Why did a small Worcestershire convent attract such powerful benefactors? One answer is its unusual affiliation – it was one of the only four English houses of the French order of Fontevrault. Today the abbey of Fontevrault is still to be found not far from the Loire, south-east of Saumur. Its magnificent church and extensive monastic buildings tell of the order's important past. In its early days the regimen was austere

1 *The kitchen and refectory of the abbey of Fontevrault.*

and simple. Robert of Arbrissel, an eccentric and holy man, had instituted the order in 1100 to bring together his followers, many of them living with him as hermits in the woods of Creon. Although the new movement may have been a welcome part of the religious renewal of the late 11th century, it is not surprising that it initially alarmed the local bishop, Baldric of Dol. Many of Robert's followers were women, some of doubtful reputation; others had deserted their homes and husbands to join him in the forest; all were drawn by his magnetic personality and charismatic preaching. To regularise the situation the bishop encouraged Robert to establish his followers in a more conventional and conventual setting by building a monastic community at nearby Fontevrault. Here the women could be safely immured in a religious life and would no longer be a target for scandal. Robert's first concern was their well-being. The new abbey was to be primarily a female house where his women followers lived under Benedictine Rule, adjusted somewhat to accommodate their original eremitical calling. Strict enclosure within the monastery was laid down and more solitude and silence than Benedict had enjoined. Partly because of the women's careful separation from the world, and partly because of the men who had joined Robert's original following, he included a male house alongside the women's, within the same enclosure. The male element was always smaller – there may have been several hundred women at Fontevrault's beginning – and, essentially, was there to serve and assist the women. To enable them to move about more freely than the enclosed nuns, the men lived as canons under the Augustinian Rule, which did not impose enclosure on its members. Later a leper house was built and the women seem to have divided into two houses, one for conversae, those who had once been married or lived as adults in the world, the other for those who had been at Fontevrault since childhood.

Robert of Arbrissel laid down that only a conversa, with her experience of the world, could be abbess. A woman was to be head of the whole foundation and she must be a sharp and knowledgeable leader as well as devout and holy. From the first the abbey attracted influential and aristocratic women. Among the early abbesses were the noble Petronilla of Chemille and a little later Matilda of Anjou, aunt of Henry II, King of England. Queens and princesses favoured it too. Eleanor of Aquitaine, Queen of England and once Queen of France, generously endowed the abbey and lived her last years there before her burial in the church, and an English princess, Mary, daughter of Edward I, was abbess at Fontevrault in 1293. Henry II must have come to know and respect the order in France, which by 1150 had grown to 70 houses, and he wanted to encourage more daughters of Fontevrault to be established in his English realm. Despite this rapid growth the order retained its reputation for holiness and a strict Rule. Such an excellent institution was to be encouraged in the king's English realm as well as in his French lands.

Thus it was politically and socially astute for the de Says to place their Westwood nunnery with prestigious Fontevrault. This move would find them royal favour and encourage donors such as the Earl of Chester and the Countess of Warwick; other early benefactors to Westwood, like Walter de Clifford who gave the priory Little Aston in Gloucestershire, also moved within the royal circle. Strangely perhaps, with Fontevrault's high reputation and kingly connections, only three other houses were founded in England: Nuneaton, established by the wealthy Robert, Earl of Leicester, later royal justiciar, and Amesbury, an old Benedictine house, refounded for Fontevrault by the king himself. There was also, for a while, a small house at Grovebury but with no lasting female element.

To endow and initiate a religious house must not only have impressed the founders' peers but more importantly brought religious merit. By this time the doctrine of purgatory was well developed; the Church was teaching that after death penitent Christian souls would go first to be judged, then on to purgatory. There, to expiate their sins, they must endure the cleansing fires for their allotted time before being deemed fit for heaven. It was a second-chance doctrine, superceding the earlier harsh belief that all were doomed to hell however blameless their lives, and that only saints, nuns, monks and the more godly priests were exempt. From the 12th century onwards the doctrine of purgatory became more elaborate. By various means, time could be knocked off the days and years in the fiery depths. Good works on earth, particularly those that promoted the faith, were considered beneficial. Thus, to found a religious house gained enormous merit and also set up a praying community who would intercede forever for the founders' souls and speed their passage through purgatory. Probably this last benefit was foremost in Eustachia de Say's mind when with Osbert and others she established Westwood Priory. She must have been well into middle age and, with the means and the motive for founding a nunnery, she was glad to achieve her end and to look forward to burial in the nuns' church, in the midst of their prayers forever. Such a burial was the privilege of many monastic benefactors, as was the right to nominate a nun to the house. In Lincolnshire, for example, when Sir Adam of Welle, benefactor of Greenfield Priory, made his will, he requested that besides a legacy to the house, his two unmarried daughters should enter the nunnery as their aunt had done before them.[4] At nearby Legbourne two daughters of the founder, Berengar Falconer, similarly entered the house as did Matilda, wife of the co-founder, Robert FitzGilbert. A man could die with a clear conscience if he knew his female dependants were safely provided for. It is surprising then that the de Says' descendants of the next century gave up this useful privilege when Eustachia's great-granddaughter, Margaret, through her husband, surrendered the right to nominate a nun to Westwood with no hint of a reason given.[5]

Osbert and Eustachia may have expected customary spiritual and temporal benefits from their nunnery and they must have felt satisfied that they had established Westwood on a reasonably sound foundation. Even if it was not flush with land and other endowments, the affiliation to Fontevrault had won powerful interest that would hopefully protect Westwood if problems ever arose. Unfortunately, some years after its founding, Westwood fell into a prolonged and acrimonious dispute with the cathedral priory at Worcester. The quarrel concerned the church at Dodderhill, not far from Westwood Priory. The nuns claimed that their founder, Osbert FitzHugh, with the bishop's blessing and that of the king, had appropriated the church to them; the monks, on the other hand maintained that it was theirs, bestowed upon them by Osbert's forbears. There must have been much dispute with documents going to and fro, since the 'poor nuns' put up strong resistance, loathe to surrender such a valuable asset. Their mother abbess at Fontevrault, Aldeburgis, did all she could to help but in the end even she had to give way to the prior of Worcester. Her letter of capitulation (1178) was a masterpiece of superior dignity in which she wrote that she was 'surprised that they [the monks] now claim the church' since they had made no objection when the nuns had received it, but 'to avoid further litigation she will observe whatever decision is reached by the bishop' and his advisors 'as strife was unbecoming to a servant of God'.[6] Thus Westwood lost Dodderhill but, out of concern for the nuns and respect for the abbess, the prior gave them in return all the land and tithes of Clerehall as well as the tithes of Crutch and Westwood, with the burial rights and offerings of the same. In the end, the nuns probably felt they had done quite well.

Cookhill

Cookhill Priory's founding seems somewhat similar to Westwood's but it is decidedly more shadowy. Like Westwood, it followed the Benedictine Rule and claimed a noble founder. The nuns of Cookhill were proud to boast of Isabella de Mauduit, Countess of Warwick, as their aristocratic benefactor, and the year 1261 as their founding date. Certainly in his will Isabella's husband, William Beauchamp, left 10 marks 'to the church and nuns of Kokeshull and Isabel my wife'.[7] Isabella, a countess in her own right, had also endowed the house and in her last years she lived there among the nuns and was buried in their chapel. Until at least the early 17th century her tomb was visible, for when Thomas Habington, the contemporary Worcestershire historian, visited Cookhill he was still able to read the broken inscription. But the countess cannot have been the original founder as much evidence points to Cookhill nunnery being at least a century older.

There is convincing written record for a mid-12th-century foundation. For example, the Pipe Rolls for 1155-6 record that the nuns of 'Cochilla' received 7s. 6d.,[8] while an entry in the Papal Register of 1400 could set a date even earlier than this. The entry concerns the request of the parishioners of Spernor (Spernall) for a licence to make a new cemetery. They argued that the one in place when the nuns were at Spernall was in a terrible state, 'being utterly destroyed and brought to the ground, the bodies ... exposed to be devoured by wild beasts', all brought about after the nuns of Cookhill abandoned the cemetery and priory and 'transferred themselves to Kochill ... distant two miles'.[9] The Cookhill nuns therefore appear to have originated at Spernall, though they may not have been there long, although long enough to build some shelter and establish a burial ground for which they could charge anyone outside the convent a useful burial fee. If they were living at Cookhill by 1155, then some time in the 1130s or 1140s would be a possible date for their original Spernall founding.

Cookhill's history becomes more certain later in the 12th century. A deed of William Beauchamp, Earl of Warwick, confirmed the gift of a church given to the nuns by his family, including his grandfather.[10] The deed is undated but must refer back to at least 1205 or before as his maternal grandfather, Waleran, Earl of Warwick, died in that year. More precisely we know that in 1227 Prioress Sarah of Cookhill disputed with two local men over the advowson of nearby Alcester parish church[11] and, more happily, that in 1241 Henry III, ever generous, gave the nuns two barrels of wine,[12] followed in the next decade by gifts of oaks for building. This new building may well have represented a revival in the nunnery, a new start encouraged by Countess Isabella, who could have found the nuns at a low ebb and renewed their impetus for the religious life. Her concern and energy were obviously important enough for her to become known as the monastery's founder.

2   *Niche in the outer north wall of Cookhill Priory church.*

The first founding of Cookhill, possibly in the 1140s, would make the nunnery more or less contemporary with Westwood and like it in having a countess of Warwick as a benefactor; thus the Cookhill nuns could also consider themselves a noble foundation. However, they had little else to compare with Westwood's grand Fontevrault connections. Most of their other benefactors seem to have been local landowners, small gentry and not of the baronial class. For example, the Durvassals, who gave the priory land in Spernal, were under-tenants of the Earl of Warwick; they shared his charitable lead but not his social rank. The one exception to the general run of Cookhill's donors is Thomas, nephew of the Earl of Gloucester, who gave the nuns a mill at Chipping Campden, whose dues would have provided a steady and valuable income. At the Dissolution the mill, with a pasture, was assessed at 19s. a year, making it a valuable asset.[13] But despite some wealthy support, poverty was to be ever present at Cookhill. The endowments of land in Cookhill and nearby Inkberrow, land at Cladswell and property at Hatch Lench, holdings at Spernall and at Tachbrook, as well as some holdings over the county border in Warwickshire, even when supplemented by financial dues and later donations of more land and property, was never enough to sustain a comfortable life for the nuns. Their nunnery was the poorest of the Worcestershire houses.

Pinley

The material situation of Pinley Priory in Warwickshire, another Benedictine house, was even worse: at the Dissolution its income reached only £25 a year compared with Cookhill's £34. Founded in Henry I's reign by Robert de Pillarton, Pinley lay not far from Warwick. Its founder was not an important man; Robert de Pillarton appears as an under-tenant of Robert de Butler, lord of the manor of Pinley. Apart from religious merit, Robert probably hoped to improve his social standing and win the regard of the local gentry by founding a monastery. Finding benefactors for his nunnery put him in touch with important people such as Waleran, Earl of Warwick, who gave the priory land and tithe corn and a further two marks in annual rent if the nuns accepted his daughter, Gundrada, and his niece, Isabel, into their community.[14] Another great lord, Robert, Earl of Leicester confirmed (*c.*1120) his tenant Ernald de Bosco's small gift of land 'to God and the church of St Mary de Pinneleg and the holy nuns there serving God'.[15] Apart from these endowments, the nuns only had lands in Pinley given by their founder, and other small parcels of land in the locality scattered around nearby manors, several of which were in walking distance of the priory. Further away, Walter D'Eiville gave them a tithe of his mill at Walton D'Eiville, but even taken altogether, these were not substantial endowments and did not make a very promising beginning.

Whiston

While Pinley and Cookhill, like Westwood, were part of the great crop of female monastic houses that characterise the mid-12th century, Whiston, Worcester's city nunnery, appeared a century later when enthusiasm for monastic founding had largely died away. The house lay outside the city, beside the road leading northwards to Droitwich and Kidderminster. Since at least the 1140s there had been a church at Whiston belonging to the cathedral priory, and much of the land was a manor of the Bishop of Worcester. This link remained. When the nuns remembered their founding, the date they celebrated was St Mary Magdalen's day, 22 July, the day in 1255 when Bishop Walter Cantelupe (1236-66) had come to dedicate their church, having confirmed his gifts of land to the house.[16] He became revered as their founder but there is evidence for the beginnings of the community in Worcester some years before his time.

In February 1240-1 when Henry III was staying at Evesham, he sent six oaks from Feckenham Forest to the 'penitentes sorores' of Worcester,[17] followed two days later by a gift of 40s.[18] Four years later more money came their way, 100s., by royal command; but now the women are noted as being 'outside' Worcester.[19] In the same years the king sent other gifts to the city's holy women: a barrel of wine in 1241 for the 'white sisters'[20] and then in 1245 10 oaks for building to the nuns of Whiston.[21] Who are these differently named women? The description white or penitent sisters disappears after 1245; all further entries in the rolls recording royal gifts refer to nuns (moniales) and usually white nuns. It seems as if the earlier sisters may have been subsumed into another female group and then transformed into nuns. Previously they had been lay sisters, but became regular religious, living in a house well beyond the city's north gate.

One reason for this change of status may have been the penitent sisters' origins. It is possible that they were part of an order for reformed prostitutes blessed by Pope Gregory IX in the 1220s. Founded in the early 13th century, appropriately dedicated

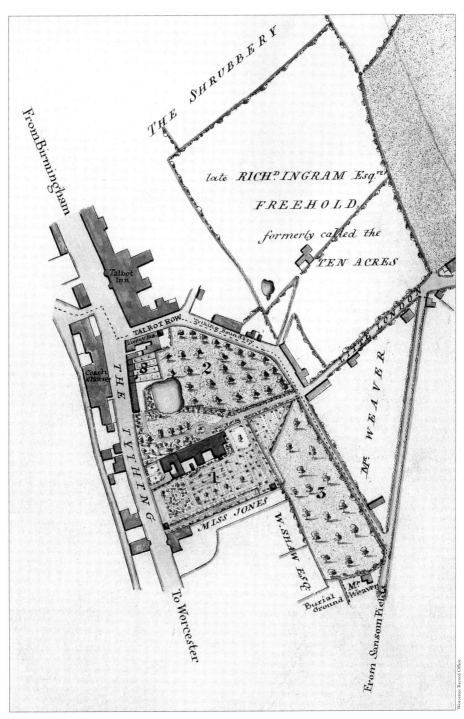

3 *Part of a plan of the White Ladies Estate from the Six Masters Survey Book (1826), showing the site of the Whiston nunnery.*

4 *Nineteenth-century drawing of the ruined White Ladies chapel.*

to Mary Magdalen, the order spread quickly. It had houses in many European cities where the members could withdraw from their old ways and from further temptation. Wearing the white robes of penitence, they could constantly remind themselves and the world of their new resolve. The 'penitentes sorores' of Worcester were most likely a part of this movement and, perhaps, as they became safely established in the city and showed commitment to their new respectable life, Bishop Cantelupe decided to re-form them into regular religious as Benedictine nuns and to give them a new home at Whiston to mark a new beginning. Here, other women with blameless origins could join them. Yet Mary Magdalen remained as their patron saint and they continued to wear white robes and were most usually called the white nuns or white ladies until the nunnery's dissolution.

Although the bishop dedicated the White Ladies' church in 1255, building on the site must have started years before. By 1257 Henry III had already sent 25 oaks to the community, including the gifts to the penitent and white sisters. In all, Henry III gave the nuns 35 oaks from his nearby forests and his son, Edward I, followed with another six. These were substantial gifts, which were markedly more than those given to the other two Worcestershire priories. Henry III was ever generous to those in need – monks, nuns, or royal servants and their families. Bishop Cantelupe too remained solicitous for the nuns' welfare. No wonder they regarded him as their founder. He added to his original donation of land in Whiston by giving them the tithes of his manor of Northwick as well as tithes owed him by tenants at Claines, both no distance from the nunnery. Further afield, the bishop gave the nuns a generous holding at his Aston manor north-east of Worcester: 51 acres of arable and two of meadow, the area that ever after has been called White Ladies Aston. Hopefully where the bishop led, others would follow. Cantelupe's care and concern for the Whiston nuns must have given them a confident beginning.

Past historians, such as those of the Victoria County History (VCH), have often categorised the Whiston nuns as Cistercian. The nuns' wearing of white or rather undyed woollen habits supports this supposition and in a few documents they are described as being of the order of St Bernard, who was the greatest figure of the early Cistercians. But it is less than likely that they were ever true members of the Cistercian order, as a closer look at the evidence demonstrates. For example, all Cistercian houses were dedicated to the Virgin Mary, yet Mary Magdalen was Whiston's saintly patron. Again, all Cistercian houses were organised in a mother-daughter relationship whereby the head of the founding mother house was responsible for all that monastery's daughter houses. Thus, hypothetically, the abbess of the house that founded Whiston should formally visit the house each year. We know that no Cistercian house features in the story of Whiston's founding and that the regular visitor was not a senior Cistercian but the bishop of Worcester or the cathedral prior. Moreover at their General Chapters in 1221 and 1228, before Whiston was founded, the Cistercians had laid down that they would accept no more female houses. Women were considered too much of a responsibility; the overseeing of their welfare and their vulnerability made them a burden for the order's superiors. Before this, a number of women's houses had become part of the order but the Cistercian leaders wanted no more. At Cookhill too, a priory dedicated to St John and St Mary, the Cistercian attribution occurs, most often in the last 50 years of its existence when it is sometimes described as of the order of Citeaux. Finally the Valor Ecclesiasticus describes Pinley Priory as Cistercian but, apart from a Dissolution document in which they are described as of 'the order of St Bernard and St Benet', there is no other reference to this supposed affiliation. What conclusion can be drawn from such conflicting evidence? Cookhill and Pinley, like Whiston, were always visited and cared for by the local bishop and there is no hint of any person from these houses travelling to Citeaux for the order's General Chapter. The best study of the problem is in Dr Sally Thompson's work, in which she arrives at the conclusion that nuns of convents like Whiston, Cookhill and Pinley and others throughout the country, because they admired the Cistercian Rule, attempted to follow it independently, although they were never official members of St Bernard's order.[22] They may have liked to be thought of as Cistercian but the Cistercian hierarchy gave them no welcome to their order.

Wroxall

In contrast to Whiston's all too human origins, Wroxall claimed a fairytale founding. Sometime before 1140 one Hugh, Lord of Hatton and Wroxall, had gone on crusade, but unluckily he had been captured and languished in prison in the Holy Land for seven unhappy years. At last he thought to pray to St Leonard, patron saint of his home church in Warwickshire and patron saint of prisoners, particularly prisoners of war; at once his fortunes changed. Appearing in the robes of a Benedictine monk, the saint told Hugh to get up and go home and there to found a nunnery. By unspecified magical means Hugh was whisked back to England to find himself arrived in the forest near his home. A bemused shepherd came across him and, despite Hugh's dishevelled, hairy appearance with fetters still rattling at his ankles, he led his lord back to his family who unsurprisingly failed at first to recognise the unkempt stranger. Soon, though, Hugh remembered to produce his half of a ring broken with his wife on his departure, and he was joyfully reunited with his wife and family. In thanksgiving, Hugh founded the nunnery and called Edith, a nun from Wilton Abbey, to teach his novices the Rule. His daughters, Cleopatra and Edith, and later probably his widow joined the house. This unusual and miraculous beginning, favoured by a saint, seems to have attracted auspicious grants from other wealthy benefactors. Besides Hugh's gifts of his lands in Wroxall, and lands and the church at Hatton, Robert, Earl of Leicester, granted the nuns rents at Hinckley.[23] This must be the same Robert who founded the Fontevrault Priory at Nuneaton, only a few miles from Wroxall but in Lichfield diocese. Robert was one of England's most powerful nobles and married to Amice, once the betrothed of Henry I's illegitimate son Richard, who drowned in the fatal White Ship. Robert was half-brother through his mother to Gundreda, Countess of Warwick, benefactor of Westwood and thus, like her, claimed descent from Charlemagne. Perhaps his brother-in-law, the Earl of Warwick, had recruited him to Wroxall's cause, as Roger of Warwick was Hugh of Wroxall's overlord and for his part generously appropriated to the nuns the church at Shuckburgh, where they already had 20 acres of land. The church was confirmed to them in 1158.[24] The king, Henry II, also played his part and granted them 10 marks yearly.[25] This gift, apart from the prestige of its origin, would be particularly useful as nunneries often had difficulties with cash flow when rents and cash dues from tenants fell into damaging arrears. Hopefully the royal contribution would arrive regularly, even when later the Sheriff of Warwickshire and the Bishop of Worcester were made responsible for its payment. The king's grant was paid until Wroxall's dissolution, by which time the nuns had received it for nearly 400 years.

Bristol

To complete the picture of monastic foundings, we should look at the Augustinian canonesses of Bristol in their priory of St Mary Magdalen. Their reported history is not extensive and we only know that their founder in 1173 was Eva, widow of

Robert Fitzharding. Her husband had been a prosperous Bristol merchant who supported Matilda in her claim to the English throne. Despite the failure of this cause, he remained astute and wealthy enough to buy estates from Matilda's half-brother, Robert, Earl of Gloucester, and later Henry II, mindful of Fitzharding's loyal support for his mother, rewarded him with the lordship of Berkeley and its estates. Thus his and Eva's descendants became the Berkeley family, who maintained continuing rights in the priory, and also in the male house of Augustinian canons that Robert Fitzharding, like his wife, had founded and generously endowed in Bristol. Husband and wife must have had a shared interest in the Augustinian order, which they took further than their founding of the monasteries, since at the end of their lives they both lived as religious: he with his canons and she as the first prioress of St Mary Magdalen's Priory. The Augustinian order had flourished in England since the late 11th century. Its male members were ordained canons following a Rule based, with some additions, on the writings of St Augustine of Hippo. Each house was independent and the Rule might vary slightly from house to house. This flexibility and its involvement in the community made it a popular order and as many as 150 houses were established in England and Wales in the 12th century. While some of the monasteries staffed and served churches in the towns, others were built in the countryside where the canons lived a devout monastic life with no parish responsibility. The two Bristol houses were urban foundations, though Eva's house lay, like Whiston, beyond the city wall, on a steep hillside not far to the north – not in the 'desert' but sufficiently distant from the city and its people to emphasise the nuns' apartness and their monastic calling. Today the buildings have totally vanished but from written and archaeological evidence we can locate the nunnery on a corner site now bounded by St Michael's Hill and Upper Maudlin Street. Robert Fitzharding endowed his house well, but the female house seems to have struggled. Although Eva Fitzharding had given her canonesses 'competent possessions', and despite some small additions from other donors, these all proved sadly inadequate, amounting to little more than the manor of South Meads at Westbury-on-Trym and a scattering of local fields and meadows.[26] As a result the house was the smallest and poorest of the Worcester houses, always struggling and ending in 1536 with an income of only £21 a year.

The Priory Buildings

Traditionally a new house would be planted and take root with a leader and 12 monks or nuns, but it is unlikely that the smaller nunneries of Worcester diocese, houses such as Cookhill, Pinley and the canonesses at Bristol, ever reached that figure in their whole 400 years. Rather, a handful of women must have come together as soon as the first buildings were ready for them. The monastic church would have been their priority besides a dormitory and living accommodation that would hopefully develop into the refectory and kitchens, the cloisters and chapterhouse, the infirmary and other buildings as soon as sufficient money and materials were at hand. The many royal gifts of oak to the nunneries tell us that most of these first buildings must have been largely of wood, or wood with an infill of wattle and daub or similar material. Gradually these may have been replaced by or enlarged into more substantial buildings. At Westwood the priory had to wait many years for an infirmary to be built, all the time managing with some makeshift arrangement, until in 1246 the prioress received a generous £10 from Eleanor, Henry III's queen, sent 'to build their infirmary'.[27] She obviously knew something of this house with its distant royal connections, as five years earlier she had sent them a Lenten gift of £2 to buy fish 'of the king's gift'.[28] As the most important buildings, the churches of the nunneries would have been built of stone as befitted the house of God. The remnants of the Whiston church are of stone, a red sandstone, as are those at Pinley and Cookhill. At Wroxall the story is more detailed, for at the beginning of the 14th century Alice Croft, one of the nuns, met Our Lady in a vision, who commanded that a new church be built. Thus work began on building a stone construction, which possibly replaced an older wood-framed building. By mid-June 1315, the work was far enough completed for Bishop Walter Maidstone to visit and consecrate the new church and the high altar.[29]

5   *Wroxall Priory church.*

6 *Fourteenth-century doorway in the north wall of Wroxall Priory church.*

As its inspirer, Alice was buried, when her time came, at the entrance to the choir – a prestigious position – and prioresses such as Dame Isabella Clinton, also privileged as founder's kin, were likewise interred within the church rather than in the monastic cemetery. Only the north aisle of this church remains today. At Wroxall, besides the church, the remains of the cloister, chapterhouse and other buildings can be seen and although we have no comparable remains for the other nunneries, nonetheless, we can make certain assumptions as to the buildings of each house. Apart from the church, there would be the frater, dorter, chapterhouse, cloister, infirmary, possibly a guest house, hopefully a warming house as well and the prioress's lodgings. Other smaller structures such as the kitchen and storerooms would have clustered around the edge of the main complex. But right from the beginning Westwood Priory had a particular building need: accommodation for the male canons who were there from the nunnery's foundation. The church, for example, would need certain adjustments. We can presume it may have been built similarly to the one at Nuneaton or to that at Amesbury, which provide two different models. At Nuneaton, where the nave had six bays, the last two were walled off to provide a chapel for the men. The dividing wall had two openings into the eastern part of the nave, probably into an ante chapel before the nuns' choir began at the third bay. There was a similar wall at Amesbury but here it was built across the choir in a position described as 'Mydquere' in 1543. Perhaps it lay a little further east than its counterpart at Nuneaton. Most likely Westwood would have followed Nuneaton in church design as the two houses were founded about the same time, while Amesbury followed 20 years later. The men not only worshipped separately but also lived at a distance from their women counterparts in their own small monastery, always known as the habit. This curious name derived directly from a Fontevrault tradition where the original male house was known as St Jean de l'Habit. At Nuneaton we know this building was situated within the outer court of the convent to the west of the church and the cloister; presumably at Westwood there would have been a similar arrangement. A habit at Westwood is mentioned but as with all the Westwood buildings we have no trace of its whereabouts.

Over their years of history the nuns must have repaired, built and rebuilt their priories many times, sometimes able to turn wood to stone as in the claustral remains at Wroxall or as at Cookhill where a new material, brick, was used for a late 15th-century range. Whatever their material, none of the Worcester nunneries was on the grand scale of some of their contemporary monastic houses, since the nunneries' modest economies precluded such ambition.

III

Cash and Kind

The management of the nunneries' estates was always a simple venture and never a great economic enterprise. While the nuns' chief aim in looking after their land and property must have been to feed and clothe themselves and their household and provide a modicum of comfortable living, they also needed to generate enough income from their estates and other assets to meet their inevitable cash expenses such as wages, building repairs, provision for new stock and seed, and also the demands for tax and fees from both Church and State. Their Rule enjoined charity and hospitality. Not only would senior churchmen and their benefactors expect to be entertained but also the house had to provide for the needs of chance travellers and the poor at their gate. Despite all these demands, the nuns might still hope for a little spare income to spend on the pleasant extras that any group of gentlewomen would enjoy.

Income in cash and kind came from three main sources: temporalities, spiritualities and occasional gifts of one kind and another. All the revenues and products of secular land and property made up the temporalities. These included rents, profits from surplus products and dues owed to a priory where it held a manor. Although they held some urban property, the nunneries' lands were mostly arable fields and pastures, some directly farmed, others leased out or held by villeins for work service. All the Worcestershire houses benefited from mills and watermills, which, despite the resident miller taking his share in kind or fees, still brought in a steady small income. Pinley, unusually, had a windmill, which stood on land belonging to Reading Abbey in the nearby village of Rowington. Consequently, every year from the profits of the mill the nuns had to pay a tithe of corn to that distant abbey.[1]

Spiritualities comprised the income derived from land and property of an ecclesiastical nature. Appropriated churches with their tithe income were the most valuable asset of this category, for as well as the 'greater' tithe of the church, the nuns also had the right to fees, such as those for burial or the dues paid to the church by a villein on inheriting his father's land. These would provide a steady income and might be fiercely defended, as witnessed in the 1367 dispute between the Cookhill prioress and the prior of Studeley over the fees from the Spernall cemetery.

Finally came the income from gifts of different kinds. These might be regularly expected, like the Crown's annual grants to Wroxall and the White Ladies, or they might be unexpected, such as a legacy or a single monetary gift. All the houses received legacies from time to time. Such gifts must have often seemed Godsent, allowing the nuns to pay wages already owed or to satisfy creditors and holding the balance between disastrous debt or financial equilibrium. A look at each nunnery in turn can tell us more about their varying economic situations.

Whiston

On the whole, although there are no surviving account rolls as evidence, the White Ladies seem to have managed their economy fairly well. They were never a rich house and their first years were difficult, with periodic crises. Early in his episcopate Bishop Giffard had had to make extra financial provision for them and some years later in 1284 he sent them, and other religious houses of Worcester, corn and barley and a money gift to buy herrings.[2] But gradually, as their property increased in the 14th century, they avoided the financial crises that other houses faced, although at the beginning of that century they did admit to having had 'to beg, to the scandal of womankind and the discredit of religion'[3] and as with other small religious houses, they were often excused taxation on grounds of poverty. Most of their holdings accumulated conveniently close to the nunnery, such as tenements in the city or land around the priory or further into the countryside. Bishop Godfrey Giffard seemed as concerned for the nuns as his predecessor Cantelupe had been. Apart from his gifts in kind, by 1301 he had bought for them, from Peter de la Flagge, 12 acres of land in Northwick and an acre of wood.[4] Some years after, in 1334-5, the nuns accepted more lands in Northwick, just north of Worcester, from William Beauchamp, Hugh de Hawford and Thomas atte Mulne,[5] not long after Joan Talbot of Richard's Castle in Shropshire had already left the priory another 15 acres of Northwick land.[6] Altogether these acquisitions brought at least 57 acres of mixed land in Northwick, a substantial holding and conveniently only a mile or so from the convent. These new holdings were especially useful in relieving the priory's debts.

Property in the city also came their way. In the early 15th century Alice Benet, who obviously had considerable property interests, gave the 'white nuns' several small properties in Worcester city.[7] She, sometimes joined with others, bestowed on them tenements, shops and land, all of which brought valuable money rents. Evidence of further small properties of the White Ladies appears in the cathedral records. For example, in 1297 we hear of a tenement in the High Street 'demised to the priory by the Will of Robert Bataylle citizen of that town' or, in 1480, of another tenement in Melcheapen Street.[8] At the Dissolution the convent's land and property were worth £33 and added to this was their income from spiritualities, another £22. The spiritualities derived from tithes on land in Claines, Northwick and Newland, all nearby; similar annual dues came from White Ladies Aston and from their appropriated church (since 1404) at Weston-on-Avon.

Clearly the prioress must have needed help in managing all this varied land and property, in farming and leasing it, gathering in rents, tithes and dues, repairing buildings, setting and paying wages; indeed everything to do with estate management. Although there is no medieval evidence of who assisted the prioress, the Valor Ecclesiasticus, 1535, lists the salaries of a steward and two bailiffs as charges on the Whiston monastic estate. Twenty shillings went yearly to John Kettilby as steward, and the same to the bailiffs, Richard Cokks and Thomas Ludlowe.[9] No doubt they and their predecessors were kept busy, particularly travelling to the further property at Weston-on-Avon in Warwickshire or at White Ladies Aston.

7   *Fields at White Ladies Aston. The Whiston nuns held lands here almost from their founding.*

Cookhill

The other nunneries had equally widespread estates. At Cookhill the furthest property held was at Condicote in Gloucestershire, many miles from the convent. It lay high on the Cotswolds, not far from Stow-on-the-Wold. The watermill at Chipping Campden with some pasture was only a little nearer but worth a journey for the steward as it brought in 19s. a year. The Cookhill nuns' other lands were largely those of their founding years, all of which lay within a few miles of the nunnery, though by 1535, they had a tiny property in Worcester that perhaps allowed the prioress an occasional visit to town. It was worth 2s. annually, contributing little to their meagre total of £16 5s. 4d. in temporalities. Their spiritualities at £19 3s. 11d., did slightly better. They were derived mostly from tithes from nearby manors such as Hatch Lench and Shyrlench and also a more substantial £13 6s. 8d. from the nuns' appropriated church at Bishampton, which must have proved a precious asset.[10]

The money was desperately needed. The Cookhill nunnery was easily the poorest of the three Worcestershire houses. Even if it named a countess as its founder and had other noble connections – Thomas, the Earl of Gloucester's nephew, had given them the Campden watermill – still the nuns' total annual income was a sparse £35 9s. 8d., leaving them with many problems. There are constant references to difficulties with taxation. In 1280 the nuns fell behind with a papal tax demand and in subsequent years the bishops of Worcester repeatedly asked that the nuns be excused taxes, such as a tenth to the Pope for a renewed crusade to the Holy Land (1300), or another tenth for Edward II's campaign against the Scots (1320).[11] In 1300 Giffard had written to the tax collectors asking that 'as poor mendicant religious the holy nuns of Wyston and those of Pynneleye and Cokhulle' should be excused from payment. The situation could not have been more straightforward: the nuns simply had not got the money. At times they seem in an alarming condition. In 1279 Bishop Giffard had to allow, for 'the relief of the nuns of Cockhulle', a special tithe of the 'sheaves and hay of the parishes of Churchlench and Hatchlench' and in 1285 Giffard ordered that only the chaplain, Thomas, should manage the nuns' financial affairs, saying such an arrangement would give the nuns more time for worship, but it must have also been an opportunity for a firmer monetary control than the nuns could ever provide.[12] By 1331 the nuns were again in crisis and they came weeping to Bishop Orleton, whose register describes them in a pathetic scene:

> From their tearful plaint he understands because of the sterility of their lands, the destruction of woods, murrain of animals and the withdrawal of alms they were wont to receive from certain great men as well as other hazards of the times, they are oppressed by such a burden of poverty that unless they received opportune assistance their monastery will be brought to the irredeemable shame of dissolution.[13]

Orleton responded with 'fatherly compassion' by appropriating to them Bishampton church, of which Cookhill already held the patronage. But even this source of funds, which in 1535 was worth £13 6s. 8d. annually, could not solve the priory's chronic financial problems. Their resources seemed totally inadequate for them to pay their way. In 1336 Edward III allowed them respite from paying a tax debt of £15 owed to the Crown because they 'were so slenderly endowed that they

8   *Bishampton church, which was appropriated to the Cookhill nuns in 1331.*

have not enough to live on,'[14] and in 1402 Cookhill was once again excused a tenth as the priory's rents were 'poor and weak'.[15] Earlier in 1353 they had run up huge debts: they owed one clerk, Geoffrey de Welveford, 40 marks and two years later their vicar at Bishampton an incredible £200.[16] It seems as if he may never have been paid since Bishop Orleton gave the nuns the church 20 years before.

Pinley

Pinley was another struggling house. The bishops' registers record several occasions when they too were to be excused taxation as 'their means are so small'. As we have already seen, kindly Bishop Giffard wrote to the collectors of a tenth for the Holy Land asking that they be excused the tax. At the Dissolution Pinley's annual income was only £23, even less than that of Cookhill, with whom they were often linked in tax exemption. Perhaps the Pinley nuns were particularly unlucky. Twice donors gained permission to endow the nunnery and twice their intention failed. In 1310 Philip le Lou and his wife sought a licence in mortmain for the nuns to gain the advowson and appropriate the church of Whatcote, and later, Thomas Beauchamp, Earl of Warwick, arranged a licence for the nunnery to have half the income of Moreton Morell church, but for some unspecified reason, neither gift materialised.[17] The Pinley nuns' poverty must have been widely known for, over the years, first in 1195, then in 1253 and 1260, the Archbishop of Canterbury, Bishop Cantelupe of Worcester and the Bishop of Norwich all resorted to offering indulgences of at first 10 days off purgatory and then 20, to those who would assist the house. Very likely Thurstan de Montfort's gift of a tithe of all the bread, beer, fish and meat used in his household was a response to the archbishop's gesture[18] (Thurstan died in 1216), and if the tithe was delivered in kind, it must have been very welcome. Later the arrangement was simplified when, in 1277, a fixed amount of wheat and barley replaced the original gift. Despite these measures Pinley's situation did not seem to improve as in the next century the house's finances were still strained. When Bishop Montacute made a visitation to the house in the difficult 1330s, he pardoned the nuns his accustomed procuration, as did Bishop Bransford three years later. However, in 1367 another of the de Montfort family, Peter de Montfort, gave the nuns some financial cheer. He had already placed his superannuated mistress, the Lady Lora de Astley, as a nun in the convent and at his death he bequeathed to each nun 10 marks and to his former love, the Lady Lora, he left 100s.[19] Despite the slightly dubious source of this money, the prioress must have felt rewarded in that, if she had a choice, she had overcome any scruples and taken in Sir Peter's nominee. Yet it brought only a small respite; 60 years on, in 1426, Pinley was again to be excused taxation because the nuns are 'much impoverished or too diminished by inundations of water, fire or other accidental causes to pay'.[20] The existence of such houses with as little income as Pinley and Cookhill was constantly precarious and they only survived with the goodwill of the bishop and support from other kindly benefactors.

Wroxall

At Wroxall, on the other hand, its founder's generous endowment seems to have established the house on a secure footing. To take a small example: when Bishop Bransford visited the priory he must have discreetly found out beforehand the nuns' economic situation, for he not only accepted their procuration but also stayed the night. This would have involved the house in some expense because officials and servants always accompanied the bishop, all of whom would need feeding and housing in appropriate degrees of comfort. At the Reformation, the Valor Ecclesiasticus assessed the priory at £78 10s. 1d., much the same value as Westwood. There is no record of worrying poverty in Wroxall's history; it never seems to have been a large house. Only nine nuns were recorded in 1381[21] and five at the Dissolution. This makes Wroxall much smaller than Westwood, where comparably 14 nuns appear in 1381 and six at the Dissolution. With a smaller number the Wroxall nuns could probably live more comfortably than those at Westwood. The latter may have been overlarge for its income as, besides the religious, there were always domestic servants and other dependants to feed and maintain. At Wroxall, for example, in 1536, apart from the five nuns, the Dissolution commissioners found as many as seven hinds and three dairy maids, as well as the local priest, who were all dependent on the nunnery; at Westwood there were 12 servants supporting five nuns and the prioress. In the same year at Bristol the numbers were equal, with a male servant and a laundress assisting the two remaining canonesses.

Bristol

Apart from a pasture and orchard near their house, most of the holdings of the Bristol nuns were small and scattered, though none at a great distance. There was a messuage at Iron Acton, a meadow at Berton, and a parcel of land at Codrington, named Magdalen's Croft. At Bishop's Moor and Weston St Lawrence they held more substantial amounts, but probably the Southmeads manor at Westbury-on-Trym was the most valuable land and it included nine acres of woodland and a share in the common land of Trydandowne (Durdham Down). By the Dissolution they also owned several small houses in Bristol and there is record of one or two gifts in wills, such as the sixpence left them by clerk William Okeborne in 1455. Even such a small amount would have been welcomed, particularly as it was in cash, always needed for paying wages or making small purchases. The canonesses must have struggled to make ends meet; perhaps it was fortunate therefore that their convent never had large numbers to support. There were only two nuns at the Dissolution and three in 1480 with one or two novices, perhaps half the number before the Black Death in 1348-9.

Why were the Nuns so Poor?

From looking at the Worcester nunneries' economic situation so far, we begin to realise that, for most, poverty was a constant threat. There were several reasons for their problems. Firstly, as women it would have been unusual for the prioresses or their deputies to have had experience in estate management before joining a monastery. Yet the prioress on election found herself responsible for overseeing a varied and scattered estate. In addition, she would very likely be lord of one or more manors although her steward would support her both in this and other management duties. All the nunneries, apart from Bristol, where there is no record, employed stewards to assist the prioress. A steward was an administrator, a manager. He would ride round the monastic lands checking on the tenants, gathering in rents and dues, organising carriage of crops to the nunnery and many other such tasks. He also might preside over a manor court if the prioress declined to do so. Below him came the bailiffs; in 1535, there were two employed at Whiston, one each at Cookhill and Pinley and Richard Shakespeare is noted as bailiff of Wroxall, and no doubt there were others who remain unrecorded at the other nunneries.

Bailiffs were the second line of management, much closer to the workforce and the small tenants than the steward was. Often a bailiff, probably born a freeman, would have proved himself as a good, reliable worker on the priory lands before being appointed bailiff, in which capacity he organised the nunnery's villeins in their service or hired craftsmen and others to work in the farm or the fields, paid them at the week's end and even laboured alongside them at busy times. Bailiffs were rent collectors too. They and the stewards were essential to the economy of every convent and many must have been stalwart supporters of the female communities with their welfare at heart, but others may well have taken advantage of the nuns' ignorance of estate management and have been slack and lazy or, even worse, creamed off some of the profits and rents for themselves. At Westwood in 1385 there is one such instance, when William Monk, an obvious scoundrel, who had been one of the canons as well as bailiff to the convent, lay in the noxious Fleet Prison, charged with failing to present the prioress with a proper account of the moneys he had received.[22]

Apart from mismanagement there were other reasons for the nuns' shaky finances. As has already been suggested, several of the nunneries were under-endowed. From their founding years onwards, they had insufficient resources in land, property and cash to support their communities, which were not inexpensive to run. After all, the nuns were gentlewomen; they expected servants to undertake all the menial work while they worshipped in the chapel, embroidered altar linen and sewed vestments for their priest, taught any resident children and in some nunneries produced beautiful manuscripts or illuminated books. In 1535, at Wroxall and Pinley, the dependent servants outnumbered the nuns; moreover, with all their tasks in the dairy, the brewhouse, the kitchen and the bakehouse, apart from cooking and laundering, the servants would develop healthy appetites, more so than the more sedentary religious. Some bishops must have realised the danger of a community living beyond its means. For example, at Marrick Priory in Yorkshire in 1252, Archbishop Walter Gray issued injunctions restricting the community from admitting new members and for further economy he also added that no visitors should stay more than one night as the nunnery's resources were so sparse.[23] They had barely enough to feed themselves let alone hungry guests. At the end of the century, the Pope, Boniface VIII, took up this theme again in his decretal *Periculoso*. As we shall see later he was concerned to rebuild the enclosure rules for holy women and he realised only too well that if the nunneries admitted too many members and thus reduced themselves to penury, then one solution was for them to go out from the convent to beg in any nearby village or town. The bishops supported him but sometimes lay patrons followed an opposing path. A favourite way of pensioning off their loyal servants was to make them corrodians in a monastic house, of which their employer was patron or founder's kin. Typically a corrodian or his sponsor would give the monastery a lump sum or a gift of land or property in exchange for boarding in the monastery for life, or sometimes there was no boarding but just a daily allowance of food and drink provided. Although the sparse Worcester records make little mention of corrodians, we do know that in 1536 there was a corrodian at Pinley and, at Westwood, Elizabeth Mounteford, described as *'vetussala'* (a very old woman), also appears.[24] But elsewhere in monastic houses they were so common that we can assume their presence in all the Worcester houses from time to time, not just in the years before the Dissolution. The situation would have been tolerable at a nunnery like Barking Abbey, a rich and grand establishment, where at the election of each abbess the king could claim a corrody, or similarly at Romsey Abbey, another royal foundation, where we read of Juliana la Despenser, a royal dependant, and her maid both being cared for till their lives' end.[25] It was a different picture at the small, poor houses, which might try to escape such a burden: witness the arrival for life of Mary Ridel at little Stainfield nunnery not far from Lincoln. Although the prioress pleaded poverty, the king would accept no excuse and she and her convent were ordered to provide the unwelcome guest with food and clothing, shoes and all necessities for the rest of her days.[26] The pitfalls are obvious. The once and for all payment was a gamble on the corrodian's length of life, for in the relative comfort and security of the monastery, he or she might live far too long. Furthermore, the corrodians encouraged another problem: the intrusion of their secular interests into the cloister.

In looking at the problems of monastic land producing enough food for its dependent community, we must take into account the limitations of medieval farming. Where today cereal seed will produce at least a tenfold crop, in the 13th century the yield would be only three- or four-fold. Moreover, for most medieval people bread was their staple food. In sufficient quantity it would provide them with the vitamins and energy needed for everyday life, but they needed to eat far more of it than anyone today. A labourer, if he was fortunate enough to have a ready supply, might devour 5lbs of bread or pottage (a thick cereal-based soup) daily. We know that the monks and lay brothers at Bolton Abbey each ate 1,000 lbs of bread or pottage a year, nearly 3lbs for each monk a day. Nearer to home, when Archbishop Winchelsey visited Worcester Cathedral Priory in 1301, he allowed each monk only a 1lb loaf each day besides his gallon of beer – but maybe they filled up on pottage or ignored the ruling as soon as their guest had departed. Probably nuns would need about the same but their servants, busy in manual tasks, cleaning and washing, brewing and baking, would be hungrier. It has been calculated that the yield of 10 acres of land would provide for a villein and his family, four or five souls, for a year. Looking then at a monastic parallel, if in a female community there were 10 nuns and possibly 10 servants or lay sisters to be fed, they would need at least 50 acres of arable land to be secure in their provisioning. On the minus side, we must remember that usually each year one-third of this land would lie fallow. On the plus side tithe corn, as provided by Church Lench and Hatch Lench for Cookhill, could hopefully make up any deficit. By the mid-14th century, the White Ladies had acquired over 100 acres of land; this should have been sufficient to support them, but as woodland and meadow were mixed in with the arable and other would-be fallow, the remaining acres would need careful farming to provide the maximum yield. Furthermore, as with all communities reliant on a single staple food, if it failed, crisis beset them.

The worst time for such problems seems to have been in the late 13th century and the first years of the 14th century. The population had risen considerably since the Norman Conquest but food production had not kept pace. Consequently corn became more and more expensive. A run of poor harvests exacerbated the problems. In Winchester diocese, for example, manor records show that in 1272, 1289 and 1297 bad weather ruined each of the harvests. At Westwood in 1306, the priory was £32 in debt, made worse by their tenants falling behind with rent and owing them a much-needed £52,[27] and at Bristol one of the few references records that at a visitation in 1307, the canonesses were excused from paying fees to the commissaries from Worcester Cathedral Priory 'on account of their poverty'.[28] At the turn of the century the situation was so dire at both Whiston and Cookhill that the nuns went out in the streets to beg. Bishop Giffard recognised their troubles, as we have seen, when in 1284 his register records him sending the Whiston nuns and other Worcester religious a quarter of corn (28 lbs) and a quarter of barley each, along with half a mark (3s. 4d.) to buy herrings.[29] Is this gift an indication that the harvest had failed that year also and that the religious communities, along with countless others, hovered on the edge of starvation? Extremes of weather characterised the time: in the next decades torrential rain and severe drought afflicted the countryside. The most difficult years must have been between 1315 and 1322 when not only harvests rotted but disease decimated the sheep and cattle. Grain prices soared. Whereas corn was 5-6s. a quarter in 1300 to 1310, by 1315 it had risen to 26s. 8d. a quarter and even 40s. in London, and many of the already malnourished populace starved,[30] suffering 'a grievous mortalitie of people so that the sicke might unneathe burie the dead'.[31] In these years before the Black Death, misfortune cut back the population and much of society struggled to survive. The nuns would be no exception. Westwood fell into debt and the community at Cookhill, as we have seen, had dire problems and from time to time all the nuns of the diocese must have had insufficient means to feed themselves adequately, let alone starving supplicants at their door. It was not an easy time. But worse, a few years later, the Black Death brought yet another crisis that resulted in irrevocable economic and social change. From the records of Westwood we have some idea how this affected at least one of Worcester's nunneries.

Westwood

Westwood Priory had never been one of the poorest houses. Its prestigious connections probably appealed to the wealthier families in the area both to enter their daughters with a generous dowry or to endow the convent with gifts of property or land. Although it was the least substantial of the three Fontevrault houses in England, among the Worcester houses it was, with Wroxall Priory, the best established. Yet, even so, the prioress, together with the heads of the other Fontevrault houses, regularly and successfully pleaded to be exempt from taxation and procurations for the king's army. In one instance, in 1270, the Patent Rolls record that Westwood, with the other English Fontevrault houses, was excused from a twentieth to be levied on the value of their possessions[32] and on another occasion in October 1405 the prioress secured a Letter of Protection from the king, Henry IV, excusing the priory from a general purveyance to provide supplies for his campaign in Scotland. It exempted the nunnery from contributing anything for his army, neither oxen nor cows nor sheep nor pigs nor horses, nor corn or hay or carts or wagons.[33] This is the most detailed of such letters but other similar orders remain within the Patent Rolls, such as one during Edward I's campaign against the Welsh, when he commanded that Nuneaton and Westwood be spared providing grain and any already taken from them should be returned.[34] However, apart from its social standing, Westwood had another advantage since, with its built-in male element, the prioress had ready made estate managers to assist and support the nuns. Indeed, this was the prior's particular task; he was to take the land-management burden from the prioress's shoulders. Although the prior was always subordinate to the prioress in the monastery's hierarchy, in estate affairs he appears almost as her equal. His name is joined with the prioress's in legal documents, despite always coming second. Thus in 1319, 'Beatrice, Prioress of Westwood and Richard, Prior of the same place with consent of the whole convent', granted a lease to 'Richard de Leche and Agnes his wife', or earlier in 1239 Annis, prioress of Westwood, had joined with Nicholas, the prior, to make a leasing agreement with Henry, son of Wiliam de Wych.[35] On one occasion at least the prior represented the convent in an entirely different role. Accompanied by the prior of Nuneaton, Robert de Sotherey was to journey to France to attend the order's General Chapter at Fontevrault. When the two men reached Dover they had to produce their licence to travel, for this was in 1344 during wartime, with much of France seen as disputed territory. Their documents proved that they had taken an oath before the king to behave well, that they had promised not to give away any of the king's secrets to the enemy and would be alert for any information that might assist the English.[36] Occasionally, however, a prior was an embarrassment rather than an aid to the prioress. One such was Richard, of whom the Patent Rolls record complains that he, 'le priour', and Geoffrey his brother, had trespassed on neighbouring land and carried away the owner's goods.[37]

On the other hand, when a prior was competent he must have been of great value to the Westwood nuns. One who particularly stands out was Richard de Greenburgh, prior in 1342. He was very experienced and obviously regarded by the mother house at Fontevrault as something of a trouble-shooter. In the difficult years of the early 14th century, he appears first as prior of Amesbury in 1318, then similarly in 1328 as prior of Nuneaton and finally at Westwood. At Nuneaton the finances had slipped into grave disorder following the 'rebellion' of the nuns over the appointment of a prioress. The Nuneaton house had wanted one candidate, whereas the abbess of Fontevrault had insisted on another. The affair rumbled on for several years, at least once flaring into violence. In the end a compromise candidate was found. When Richard had sorted out troubled Nuneaton, he moved on to Westwood where he again set to work on the finances. By 1350, as Berenice Kerr has shown, he had raised the rent component of the priory's cash income from 20 per cent to about sixty-five per cent, a creditable achievement.[38] The prior of Westwood, among other obedientaries, kept his own accounts and a certain amount of the priory's incoming funds may well have been earmarked for his use, as they were for the chaplain whose own account roll survives for 1382-3.[39] The account rolls covered varying lengths of time; that of Prior Robert Sotherey runs from May to September 1350;[40] others, such as bailiffs' rolls, account for as long as a year. We cannot know if different obedientaries such as the cellarer or sacrist had their own 'departmental budgets' at the other Worcester female houses, as no account rolls survive.

The holdings of Westwood were as widespread and varied as any other monastery. As far away at Little Aston in Gloucestershire, the nuns held a messuage of land and nearer at hand they had added to their original endowment with lands in many places, such as Hadzor, North Piddle, Wychbold, Ombersley, Salwarpe, Hanbury and Huddington. More distant from the convent they held lands at Cotheridge, as well as the church, and two manors at Rock, land more bleakly set high above the river Teme, beside the Wyre Forest. In Bromsgrove and Droitwich, Westwood owned urban property and they also held three mills, two near the nunnery and one more distant at Martley. But it was salt that made Westwood's economy distinctive. This, perhaps, is hardly surprising as the house lay within a mile of Droitwich's substantial salt workings. Below medieval Wych, as today, lay an extensive and seemingly limitless brine deposit. In the Middle Ages this was worked by sinking

9 *The ancient porch doorway of Cotheridge church. The church was a founding endowment of Westwood Priory.*

wells into the brine layer, hoisting the liquid to the surface and then boiling the brine to retrieve the salt. It was a large-scale business; fortunes were made from salt extraction and traders distributed the precious commodity far and wide. Salt was taken in all directions from the town, but particularly to the river Severn, where boats could transport the salt northwards to central England, or south to the sea and then round the coast to London or even across the Channel to Europe.

10   *Conjectural drawing of salt-working in Wych, a brine pit to the left and a brine-boiling place on the right.*

From their foundation the nuns had owned a salinarium, a saltworks at Wych, and as time went on they acquired other salt holdings. For instance, Alicia Senne gave them a messuage in Wych that brought with it a share in the salt dues, the tax paid locally on salt.[41] Although the priory gained from salt, they also had to pay out in salt: they sent a *mitta*, a basket of salt, every Michaelmas to the Lord of Claverley and six small baskets of salt to Deerhurst Priory.[42] Despite having to give some away, their income from salt was still a precious asset. The value of salt acquired or income from it far outweighed any they had to expend. Berenice Kerr has calculated that by 1535, 22 per cent of the priory's assets at farm came from salt.[43] Also, Westwood's bullaries, salt-boiling places in Wych, made up one of the nuns most lucrative investments, bringing in 66s. 8d. annually. In about 1400 it appears that at least one of these bullaries was worked directly by the priory, as shown by the account roll of John Woodeward, 'surveyor of a bullary of salt water belonging to the prioress and convent of Westwood,' which still survives among the Hampton Papers.[44]

The invaluable Hampton archive also explains much about Westwood's monastic economy. Of the six Worcester nunneries Westwood is the only one where account rolls remain. The rolls enable us to see where the money went: we can follow wages of all sorts being paid to craftsmen and labourers, to shepherds and cowherds, to the hinds and domestic servants. Materials had to be bought for repairing buildings, beasts replaced and rents and dues met. These last could be in kind, such as a pair of white gloves given each Easter to Osbert Bende's heir in exchange for part of his land that the nuns held in Wych, although to complicate matters Bende's heir was himself a tenant. He held the said land in his turn from Deerhurst, which also entailed the nuns in regular small money payments to that priory. More expensive was the silver mark they agreed to pay to Ralph Hacket in exchange for small parcels of land, which was in addition to the 3s. they already paid him each St Andrew's Day for 'unam dalam salsae cum salina' ('one measure of saltwater with a brine boiling place').[45] There must also have been domestic expenses, although so much of what they needed was home-produced, as well as ecclesiastical needs, such as expensive wax for candles for the church, which in 1337 cost seven pence a pound. The sacrist, backed by the chaplain, would consider such a purchase essential – in God's house smokey tallow candles would not do.[46] A more mundane payment was for the iron needed for repairing tools and ploughshares, and ready-made nails also frequently appear in the nunnery accounts. One payment the priory was spared, because of its particular origin, was the fee to the bishop or cathedral prior, which the other Worcester houses regularly paid. As a house of Fontevrault, Westwood was not under local episcopal jurisdiction. Thus they evaded payments such as visitation or election fees that the other nunneries had to find. Instead they would have expected to pay dues to their abbess in France, or she may even have visited the nunnery on one of her many recorded journeys to England, although no report of her visiting Westwood remains. However, commissaries came in her place. In May of 1315 Elias, prior of the leper hospital at Fontevrault, crossed to England and was given safe conduct until Christmas 'to visit the houses of her (the abbess's) order in the realm'. Three years later another Fontevrault prior, Stephen, followed on the same mission, this time being allowed a year to fulfil his task.[47]

As always, it was easier to spend money than to make it. No doubt in good years the prior or bailiff at Westwood could collect rents and dues with some ease but this would not always be the case. Other studies show how frequently monastic tenants fell behind with their rent, particularly if they were distant from the priory. For instance the Hartlepool tenants of Marrick Priory, a north Yorkshire nunnery, owed that house £5 in 1415-16, while the total arrears for all the priory's rents for the year was £22, a massive sum.[48] Very likely at Westwood and the other Worcester nunneries, unpaid rents were a similar problem. Indeed, we have seen that at Westwood rents and moneys owed in 1306 amounted to £52 in arrears. It seems that in the difficult times of the late 13th century many tenants had not paid their full rent for many years. At Westwood the prioress was lord of the manors of Westwood, Clerehall and

Crutch and of Stillindon and Holyne in Rock. In fulfilling this role she held manor courts at which she or perhaps more often the prior or possibly the steward would preside. Some of the court rolls survive. Here, disputes between lord and tenant, or tenant and tenant would be settled and dues and fines laid down. These might include the heriot, an entry fine of money or kind, that all villein tenants would have to pay when a son inherited his father's holding. Similarly, on marriage merchet must be paid and countless other exactions caught the feudal tenant at all stages of life. No tenant would pay them willingly and no doubt in difficult years, such as between 1315 and 1322, or at the time of the Black Death, some fees went forever uncollected.

These plague years must have brought crisis of every kind to the nunneries. From the Westwood rolls we can gather some idea of the impact it made. They do not, of course, tell specifically of the misery and fear the great plague brought, although there is a hint of that at Whiston. Wherever the disease struck, up to 30 per cent of the people died, leaving a disastrous shortage of labourers. Those remaining were suddenly empowered as their skills and labour were in short supply and they rapidly gained the confidence to bargain for higher wages. The account roll of Prior Robert Sotherey of Westwood, kept for four months in 1350, opens a window on the post-plague world.[49] He records the wages of John Walsh, a ploughman at Crutch, as being 18s. 4d. for 20 weeks, 11d. a week, which compares with an average 6d. a week before the disaster. Wages stayed high. In 1337, the thatcher and carpenter at Westwood Manor earned a penny a day: in 1393, their descendants took home a welcome 14d. a week, more than a 100 per cent rise.[50] This must have created problems for the prior and prioress, for their income had not risen to match the escalating wage bill. With the buying and selling of stock it is hazardous to compare like with like, as the quality and age of animals are unknown, but it seems that the prices paid for stock remained roughly the same. For example, in 1393 Westwood Manor bought a pair of oxen for 18s. and another pair for 2s. less, yet in 1337 they had bought two oxen for 21s.; in this case it seems the price had actually dropped. But were they all comparable beasts? We can never know. Furthermore, with fewer free tenants wanting land, rents could scarcely be raised and with fewer villeins surviving there would be less income from rents and dues, besides which, on the 'spiritual' side, the tithes would drop in value as a lower population would need less food grown. Although the population gradually rose again, the social clock was never to be turned back to the pre-Black Death society. Many villeins had taken the chance of a strong bargaining position to become free tenants and thus the shape of the manor hierarchy changed forever. There are indications that in the opening years of the 15th century the nunneries again faced severe economic hardship. Were the royal grant of £10 yearly given to Whiston in 1400 and the bishop's appropriation to them of the church at Weston-on-Avon in 1407 answers to pleas of exceptional hardship?[51] This was also the time when the same king, Henry IV, spared Westwood nunnery his purveyance and exempted Cookhill, Pinley and Wroxall from taxation; Cookhill because their rents were 'poor and weak'.

In time the nunneries seem to have recovered from this particular storm. At the Suppression Pinley had debts but none are recorded at Bristol or Wroxall. The sad reduction in numbers of nuns after the Black Death must have helped – the White Ladies lost two-thirds of their house, reducing in number from 18 to six – and possibly something of the increasing prosperity of the town economies would have flowed their way. Unfortunately we can never be precise about the Worcester priories' financial problems as no account rolls survive except at Westwood, and even there they are insufficient to give a complete picture. Their difficulties sprang mainly from inadequate original endowments, and despite later acquisitions of churches, land or property, they never had enough. They constantly needed more cash flow but this was beset with difficulties, not least that up to the Black Death they may have admitted more nuns than their resources could sustain and consequently lived beyond their means. Berenice Kerr has calculated that in 1340, when she thinks Westwood may have held 50 nuns, the priory would have needed £253 a year to support them.[52] The other houses, being smaller, would need less but their solvency still depended on rents and dues being paid on time and occasional gifts and bequests coming their way. It was a precarious existence, yet with the goodwill and support of their bishops and the Crown, when crises threatened, the six houses of Worcester diocese managed to avoid humiliating financial collapse and to remain open to the end.

IV

Life in the Nunnery

Within the walls of the Worcester nunneries the basic pattern of life continued as it had done since Benedict's day as a round of work, worship and rest. Quite a lot can be uncovered about the women who followed the Rule, their family backgrounds and why for many it was a fulfilling life, but why for others the sheer predictability of their days pushed them into forbidden ways. For a number of reasons, most medieval nuns sprang from the gentry class in society. Occasionally they came from the nobility and even more occasionally, as at Fontevrault, from royalty itself.

Interestingly, a nunnery often echoed the stratifications of medieval society with the prioress, the authority figure, socially superior to the other nuns, coming from a powerful local family. Ideally such a woman, used to a large household and estate, would have the self-confidence and experience of management to run the monastery with its people and land efficiently and well. A prioress of high social standing was characteristically found in the English Fontevrault houses, who took their pattern from the mother house where the earliest abbesses numbered women such as Matilda of Anjou, widow of Henry I's heir, who drowned in the White Ship. Westwood could not compete with this grandeur but all the same at least two of their prioresses came from notable families. One was the 13th-century Benedicta de Clifford, probably descended from Walter de Clifford, one of the original benefactors of the priory, and she also must have been related less reputably to Fair Rosamund Clifford, famed paramour of Henry II. Isabella Russell, elected prioress in 1405, also came from a distinguished background: the Russells lived not far away at Strensham and one in particular, Sir John Russell, was a close advisor to Richard II. Such prioresses, it was hoped, would attract support and gifts to the nunnery and their family influence might be useful with royal and local officials to allay taxation demands or solve legal disputes. At Wroxall as well, founder's kin played their part. The founder Hugh's heirs were the de Clintons, a powerful local family, and we find two de Clinton ladies as prioresses of Wroxall in the 14th century. One, Isabella, played on her status, creating a lot of trouble before she achieved leadership; the other, Alice, seems to have been a quieter character. None of the prioresses we know of at the other Worcester nunneries would have had the same social standing as a Clifford or a Russell, yet Alice Flagge of Whiston, prioress in 1308, would undoubtedly have had local prestige. The Flagges appear to have been well-heeled Worcester landowners, able to sell surplus land to the bishop and with strong church connections. Their name is still found in the city, where the playing field Flagge Meadow, once owned by the Whiston nuns, may well have been land brought to the convent by Alice as her dowry. A dowry, although forbidden by Saint Benedict, was by now a well-established requisite of entry to monastic life and it was, of course, another reason why only women with money behind them could join a nunnery. At Laycock Abbey, for instance, Berenice Kerr calculates that Joan Sambourne's family must have spent at least £12 in equipping her for monastic life; she needed clothing and bedding as well as her cup, bowl and spoon.[1] Today's equivalent to this £12 cost in 1395 would be several hundred pounds. Yet all was not lost for poorer entrants, for in some houses

11 *Flagge Meadow in Worcester. Alice Flagge may have brought it to the Whiston convent when she entered the house in the late 13th century. Today it is school playing fields.*

they would be accepted as lay sisters. These women and girls took the monastic vows but their daily round was mostly spent, as with their male equivalents, in the heavier manual work both indoors and out, and consequently they were not free to attend all the offices. When they did attend, they were seated in the church separately from the choir nuns. In the largest religious houses their separate accommodation for eating and sleeping reinforced their second-class status, but in the small Worcester female houses a separate dorter and refectory for the needs of lay sisters seems unlikely.

Apart from the prioresses we can also put together something of the family background of other less exalted Worcester nuns. Although Westwood Priory may have ranked low in the Fontevrault hierarchy, among the Worcester houses it would have stood high. After all, at the mother house in France, great noblewomen, princesses and retired queens, such as Eleanor of Aquitaine, had been professed and at their sister house of Amesbury, Eleanor, widow of Henry III, her daughter Beatrice and her granddaughter Mary had been nuns. Westwood may have boasted of such connections but its nuns, as far as we know, were not in the grandest league. They ranged from daughters of the local gentry, such as Isabella and Agnes Cassy or Edith Hornyold, to women only distinguished by their former domicile, such as Alicia de Feckenham or Margareta Hanbury. Thomas Cassy was Lord of Hadzor,

12   *Eleanor of Aquitaine, her effigy in the abbey church at Fontevrault.*

no distance from Westwood, and the Hornyold family still live in Worcestershire today. The few names known for the Whiston nunnery give hints of slightly different origins since, due to the expansion of town society as the years went by, the recruiting base widened and we find women from an urban background, from the expanding merchant class, joining the convent. Such was Katharine Goldsmyth, who was one of the three nuns at Whiston in 1485 petitioning for the election of the new prioress, whose name must describe her family's calling. Another earlier entrant with urban connections was Helena Ryons, who was professed at Whiston in 1307. Her father, Sir William, later became bailiff of Gloucester, an important post in the city. He was also a knight and several other daughters of the knightly class can be traced at the nunneries. When Helena arrived at Whiston, her companion and sister recruit was Margaret Fizier, whose father was Sir Hugh Fizier of Gloucestershire. Another Whiston nun was Alicia Lestormy, who joined the house in 1329 and is described as the daughter of Sir Robert Lestormy. In contrast, another name appears among Whiston's electing nuns in 1349, that of Ellen Spelly. She could be from a much more humble background if she was related to Osbert Spelly, a local man whom the bishop made a freeman in 1327 and subsequently 'superintendent' of five of his manors including Whiston. Osbert is also recorded as a juror at the Worcester Assize, as a legal witness in the episcopal manor at Hanbury and as buying a tenement worth 10s. in Northwick in 1343. If Osbert was Ellen's father, they were obviously a family with aspirations.

Among Wroxall's nuns and prioresses were several d'Abitots, who would be descended from Urse d'Abitot, a powerful Norman baron who had supported Duke William in 1066 and became sheriff of Worcestershire after the Conquest with lands to match. Margery, Hugh the founder's granddaughter and heir, married as her second husband John d'Abitot after the death of Osborne de Clinton, her first spouse. These marriages gave both important families an interest in the nunnery and, in the early 14th century, we find Sibilla d'Abitot as Wroxall's prioress (elected 1285), while Avicia and Alice d'Abitot were both nuns at the convent. Jumping on two centuries, one name stands out at Wroxall, that of Johanna Shakespeare, the sub-prioress in 1525, who appears again at the Dissolution when she was dispensed from her vows of poverty and obedience to return to secular life. It is intriguing to speculate how closely she might be related to William. The Shakespeares were a prolific family. In the 16th century they were found as yeoman farmers in 34 Warwickshire towns and villages, of which many were no distance from Stratford. Certainly in 1542, two Shakespeares, Richard and William, tenanted lands formerly belonging to the priory at Wroxall. Of these two Richard is almost certainly the Richard Shakespeare recorded by the Valor Ecclesiasticus as bailiff of the priory, and may be the Richard who was a monastic tenant in 1525 and bailiff of the priory's manor at Hatton, where a late 15th-century nun of Wroxall, Joan Shakespeare, was buried in the church. Could he be the sub-prioress's brother or father? Could he be the same Richard recorded as a yeoman in Snitterfield, six miles or so from the priory, 10 years later, who moved to

Stratford about 1551 and died there about 1560? This Richard Shakespeare was the poet's grandfather, and thus through this relationship Johanna Shakespeare, nun of Wroxall priory, might be William Shakespeare's aunt.

Lists of electing nuns and other documents relating to the prioresses' elections provide many of the nuns' names, as do extant lists of the names of nuns being professed, one surviving at Westwood and one at Wroxall. Where there is a sequence of election lists it is possible to gather other interesting information; one area is the surprising longevity of some of the nuns. For example, Eleanor Acton appears on two of the Westwood lists, the profession list of 1337[2] and an electors' list of 1384.[3] With the caution, as in all cases, that the same name may not mean the same person, if Eleanor was about sixteen at her profession then she must have been at least 64 in 1384. But Isabella Cassy easily exceeded this. Her name first appears as being professed in 1337, then as an elector in 1384 and again in 1405.[4] By the second election Isabella must have been at least 84 or 85 years old with 70 years of convent life behind her. Examination shows a similar picture among the Whiston White Ladies, where two election lists survive from a century later. Here Margaret Sturmy was the last named, most junior elector in 1427[5] – she could have been born around 1410 – but she survived to head the list in 1485[6] for Johanna Morton's election as prioress, by which time she must have been at least seventy-five. A handful of other nuns at Whiston lived to about sixty or beyond: Helena Ryons, who survived the Black Death, was one, Elizabeth Wootton another. Elizabeth became prioress at well over 60 in 1472 but as she died within the year, she might have been wiser to have refused the burdensome office. Other studies have also refuted the myth that all medieval people died young; they show that if a person could survive infancy, childhood and adolescence, then he or she had a good chance of reaching 50 or 60 years. Nuns of course did not have to endure childbirth, one of the great killers of women. They also had a simple diet, regular hours and no great stress. If a nun could willingly accept the Rule and accommodate the foibles of her companions, if she could develop a genuine devotion to her faith and adjust to her circumscribed existence, then she would live a contented life, another well-known recipe for longevity.

It is easy to assume that monastic women lived in a world entirely cut off from the opposite sex, but this was not so. Every nunnery had its chaplain to celebrate the daily Mass and a confessor is sometimes mentioned, who may have been a different priest. Then there was the priory steward who must have come in and out to report to and consult with the prioress. Other more lowly servants would be around, such as labourers working on the home farm or handymen and workmen looking after the monastic buildings and the precinct grounds; the Dissolution documents describe them as hinds. More exciting male visitors would arrive from time to time, whether they be founder's kin or other benefactors claiming hospitality, or church officials sent by the bishop, or cathedral prior, or even those great men themselves. While we know that the nuns often came from the landowning or merchant class, it is not as easy to pinpoint the backgrounds of their male associates. Often only a forename describes the men: Thomas, the chaplain at Cookhill, Hugh and Roger and Goodman, chaplains at Whiston. Where there are family or descriptive names we may learn a little more. Richard Crump, another chaplain of Whiston, was probably a local man as Crump is still a Worcestershire surname and Richard of Claynes is obviously from the near neighbourhood, but who are John de Warton, entertained too closely by the prioress of Wroxall, or Robert Dorning, chaplain of Whiston? The stewards of the priory lands appear as social equals to the prioresses but their chaplains seem to be lesser mortals, run-of-the-mill priests, glad to share something of the security of monastic life. The origins of the priors and monks at Westwood are a little similar to the chaplains. However, there are no obvious local ties; indeed at first they come from much further afield. Richard Normand and Robert Douet of the mid-13th century must be French, while Richard Grenebugh and Robert Sotherey a century later may have English names but they are not of the Westwood locality. Whatever their first environment though, the priors at least must have been men of some education and with management skills if they were to be of effective assistance to the prioress in running the priory.

Little precise evidence remains of how the Worcester nuns spent their days, but we can build up a picture from what was general at the time. The monastic horarium, the eight religious offices, created the framework of their lives. They rose in midnight darkness for Matins and Lauds, then returned to their beds until Prime at sunrise. Terce, Sext and Nones interspersed the middle day and Evensong and Compline completed it. As well, their chaplain regularly celebrated Mass for all to attend. However, a nun might be excused a midday office if she was busy supervising the brew house or tending a sick patient or doing other important tasks. Undoubtedly the nuns would have spent time on light manual work as well as in devotion – St Benedict had insisted on this all-important balance. Spinning was a task for all medieval women and for the nuns sewing and embroidery would also take up their time. Not only were their habits and their headdresses to be made, but household linen and fine cloths and vestments for the church had to be sewn. In some nunneries beautiful books were created, but there is no evidence for this skill in Worcester. However, they certainly had young boarders. We know that at Pinley, Earl Waleran, a founding benefactor, entrusted his daughter, Gundrada, and his niece, Isabel, to the nuns' care, providing two marks a year to cover the extra expense.[7] At Westwood too there may well have been young boarders; it was common at the sister house of Amesbury and at Nuneaton a 'pupil' is noted. Such girls must have been well looked after by the childless nuns and, as well as being taught to spin and sew along with simple reading and writing, the expectation would be that when the time came, they too would be professed in the religious life and remain within the convent walls forever. It is difficult to assess how well educated the nuns were, whether their literary skills went beyond elementary reading and writing. The daily services would demand the ability to read but some might get by with copying others or by the familiarity of repetition and, after all, as most was in Latin, there would be little incentive to improve. There is hardly a trace of any monastic library among the Worcester nunneries, and solely a hint of books at Westwood, where a copy of William of Malmesbury's *Life of St Wulstan* was found within the same manuscript as the cartulary of the priory. The more affluent Fontevrault houses at Amesbury and Nuneaton certainly had books, one of which, the *Nuneaton Book*, with its varied contents both secular and religious, is in the Fitzwilliam Museum collection.

The busiest nuns were the obedientaries, those holding official posts who would usually be well-occupied. In the church the precentor ordered the endless services, those for every day and the more elaborate liturgies for the great festivals and saints' days. Working closely with her, the sacrist found the candles and the cloths, the books and vestments, everything needful for dignified worship of God. In the house the cellarer supervised the housekeeping, a particularly responsible task. She ordered and organised the provisions and directed the servants in their work. A chambress looked after the nuns' clothing and household linen. Poor though they often were, the nuns still had duties of charity and hospitality; thus the almoner would provide for the poor, passing on worn clothing and any spare food, while the guest mistress's task was to welcome visitors and travellers begging a night's rest. The Valor Ecclesiasticus shows that at both Pinley and Wroxall certain moneys were dedicated to providing hospitality. It was hoped too, that the infirmarian would be another kindly nun, caring for the old and sick of the house as well as advising those living around the nunnery. Often, especially in the smaller houses, two or more of these posts might be combined. One nun, for example, could be precentor and sacrist, another both almoner and guest mistress. Where tasks had an overlapping element, as in preparing for the church services, such an arrangement might also avoid contentious boundary disputes between rival office holders.

Of all the monastic offices the prioress's must have been the most demanding. A successful prioress or abbess must be a leader; she needed skills for managing both people and estates. She must also earn the respect of her community and be able to represent them authoratively to the outside world while at the same time be known for her piety and holy living. As with many smallish communities the character of the leader set the tone of the whole body. Some prioresses, like Agnes de Bromwich of Whiston, were obviously confident and able. When she received Archbishop Winchelsey's visitation summons to attend him at Worcester Cathedral with other monastic heads and clergy, she refused the invitation with the retort that 'it was unseemly for women to mingle in such a company of men'.[8] She sent her chaplain instead. She must have known that her nuns' benefactor, Bishop Giffard, was hostile to the archbishop's visit and would not meet him at the cathedral, and clearly she followed suit. Other prioresses, such as Agnes de Aylesbury at Wroxall, were failures, allowing their houses to fall into disrepute. Many must have fallen between these two extremes. To become a prioress or her deputy could be a fulfilling career for a medieval woman, for, although women could hold land, be churchwardens and be involved in trade, a successful prioress or abbess had a higher standing in the community. She would have spiritual as well as temporal authority. With the aid of a steward and bailiffs she would oversee the monastic lands, receive tithes and rents, agree to new leases, worry about property repairs and difficult tenants and face adversities such as floods or inadequate harvests. In the convent she would dispense hospitality to important guests and, less enjoyably, deal with all sorts of official administration, maybe resisting royal or papal taxation or approving a priest for one of the priory's appropriated churches. Most tiresome must have been internal disputes among the nuns, inevitable at times in any small single-sex community.

The sub-prioress came into her own during an interregnum, the vacancy when the former prioress had either died or retired. She would now be responsibile for running the house, entertaining visitors and overseeing all the formal business, particularly initiating the election of a new prioress. This, with the exception of Westwood, involved much toing and froing and connection with episcopal officers or with the prior of Worcester during a vacancy in see. At Alice Flagge's election at Whiston in 1308, Lucy de Solers, the sub-prioress, was one of the prime movers for expediting the business, in which she dealt with the bishop elect as well as the prior when she anxiously pushed the matter forward.[9] About the same time, an election at Wroxall appears more enjoyable as it involved the excitement of a journey to London for the sub-prioress, Alicia de Philibert, with two other nuns, Anabel de la Mar and Alice de Craft. Once there they presented the bishop's officer with their nomination for prioress, the ill-omened Agnes de Aylesbury, and all was duly agreed and her election confirmed.[10] For the three travellers the journey through unfamiliar countryside to reach the crowded streets and houses of the city must have been an amazing contrast to their quiet life at Wroxall. At Westwood the sub-prioress's responsibilities in a vacancy were less. Officially the mother abbess at Fontevrault chose the heads of the daughter houses, though she no doubt might accept suggestions as to candidates from the sub-prioress on the spot. However, when there was a conflict of opinion, such as that between Fontevrault and the nuns at Nuneaton over their choice of prioress in 1318, a full-scale row could erupt.

For the prioress and her deputy and often for the obedientary, the office-holding nuns, convent life held responsibility and interest, but for the other women the unvarying routine must have become unbearable at times and any diversion welcome. Thus mealtimes would have made a welcome break in the day with the most substantial meal taken at midday and a light supper in the early evening. Like most medieval people the nuns existed on an unexciting diet. For them, bread and pottage provided calories and protein, supplemented by vegetables such as leeks and cabbage, beans and peas often cooked in a broth, as well as seasonal fruits. Long before, St Benedict had laid down a largely vegetarian diet but the centuries had weakened this rule. Fish was always allowed and meat from doves, chickens and other fowls. At all the Worcestershire nunnery sites fishponds are known; at Cookhill and Westwood they are still there and still fished. At Whiston, close to the river Severn,

13   *Monastic pools at Cookhill Priory.*

not only would their own fish be available but also river fish and sea fish, brought upriver and sold on the quays. We know that they ate herrings, for in 1284 they were to be part of Bishop Giffard's gift of food,[11] and at other nunneries a variety of fish including cod, salmon, pilchards, bream and eels was eaten. Gradually regular meat-eating had crept in as Benedict's strictures were forgotten, and although the women religious probably ate far less than some of the over-indulgent abbots and priors of later monasticism, we can assume they enjoyed beef, pork and mutton, enhanced with herbs and spices. Indeed the accounts of Westwood in 1338 and 1350 indicate that a calf was eaten on Trinity Sunday and young pigs at other times.[12] Much of the meat may have been preserved with salt and would then need to be cooked with the herbs and a spice such as cumin to improve its tired flavour. Meat had always been allowed for invalids; indeed at Wroxall in 1323 Bishop Cobham reprimanded the prioress and nuns for not giving the sick in the infirmary sufficient meat to speed their recoveries:

47

(they) have been robbed of their customary portion of beer, meat and fish, four nuns receiving scarcely a pint of very weak beer each day, and meat and fish and other necessaries being given in such small portions as to be scarcely enough to live on.[13]

Probably the home farm of the nunnery, besides the vegetable garden and orchard, provided most of the fresh produce including a limited amount of cheese and eggs. Although there are no records of vegetable gardens at the Worcester nunneries, they are certainly in evidence at other contemporary houses.

For drink, the nuns depended on weak ale, brewed in their own brew house from home-grown barley or that supplied by tenants. The ale might be warmed in the winter to provide a more comforting drink for the chilly nuns. However, occasionally the nuns enjoyed the rare pleasure of wine with a meal – such a luxury depended on generous royal gifts, as when in June 1241 Henry III instructed his bailiff at Tewkesbury to send each of the Worcestershire nunneries a substantial supply of wine. The other nunneries outside the county were not included on this occasion but years later in 1386, the young King Richard II granted Prioress Elizabeth Wodecroft of the Bristol convent 'a tun of red wine of Gascony yearly at Christmas' for her life's span, which must have brought great cheer to the small indigent house.[14] To conclude, an entry from the 1440 bishop's visitation to Lincolnshire's Legbourne priory sums up well a nun's typical diet:

> every nun has one loaf, one half-gallon of beer a day, one pig a year, eighteenpence for beef, every day in Advent and Lent two herrings and a little butter in summer and sometimes two stone of cheese a year and eighteen pence for raiment and no more.[15]

The last item on this list, 18d. a year for clothing, does not seem over-indulgent, nor should we expect it to be since monastic clothing was not to reflect fashion in any way but to be serviceable, long-wearing and suited to the season. In the beginning Benedict ruled that the women should have a tunic with a belt, two cowls, shoes and stockings as well as a handkerchief, a knife, a needle and writing equipment. Soon the nuns' wardrobe must have increased; this was essential as soon as monasticism spread to colder northern Europe, far from the sunshine of central Italy. In the mid-12th century the author of the Ancrene Rule gave thought to suitable clothes for one group of religious women. He was writing most probably for a small number of anchoresses living in the remote Herefordshire countryside near Limebrook nunnery and perhaps some similar garments, as he suggested for them, might have been favoured by the Worcester nuns not so far away. He recommended to his anchoresses the warm dress of the Premontre sisters. This included a tunic of wool or linen, a cloak of lambskin and woollen cloth, which could be separated in the summer for cooler wear, a black linen veil with a warm cap underneath and, handily, a small knife in a sheath. Variations on this basic outfit in the same materials, linen, wool and fur, are found for most female religious. Where undergarments are mentioned, warmth rather than hygiene is the priority. If they must, the anchoresses could wear breeches of hair cloth, although the author seems to imply that these were unnecessary, perhaps considering them effete, but he was happy with a *stamin*, a coarse woollen undergarment and a *camisia*, a shift of linen or wool.[16] The Augustinian canonesses at Lacock, another source of information, must have been more warmly comfortable in undergarments of fur, though this must surely refer to something worn beneath their habits in winter, rather than the equivalent of modern underclothes. At night the canonesses went to bed in 'a robe, and girdled … and whoever wishes may wear hosen without feet'.[17] Their bedclothes were to be a woollen or linen sheet with a pillow of down, and the Ancrene Rule specifically allows as much bedding as the anchoresses might need for warmth. The strange instruction for footless leggings must have been devised to conform with the nuns' ascetic custom of going barefoot or at least having no foot covering beyond shoes. Incidentally, the author allowed his nuns to keep a cat but decreed that other pets would encourage vanity!

Despite every order's directions for wearing appropriate clothing in sober colours and simple cloths, almost from Benedict's day nuns broke the sartorial rules. The temptation of bright colours, silks and gauzes, the glitter of silver and gold, the lure of fashion, was too much for them. As early as the late seventh century holy women were seen in violet linen 'vests' and scarlet tunics, or with their sleeves striped with silk or with coloured headdresses setting off hair crimped and curled around their faces. Such lapses constantly continued and bishops repeatedly scolded the women for their unsuitable dress. It seems that, rather like schoolgirls forced to wear uniform, some nuns valiantly tried to adapt their regulation clothes to mirror the latest fashion, thus adopting trains or widening their gowns around the hem or, as Bishop Alnwick of Lincoln noticed in 1445, when high foreheads were in vogue, the nuns at Goring Priory wore their veils 'spread out on either side and above their foreheads'. In response he 'enjoined upon the prioress … that she should wear and cause her sisters to wear their veils spread down to their eyes'.[18] The Worcester nuns had similar lapses. In 1365 Bishop Wittesley sent a letter to all the nunneries in the diocese reprimanding the inmates for various faults, including their less than sober monastic dress. His words show how far some of the religious had slipped from the Rule, as they were obviously enjoying themselves wearing:

> gauzy silken veils, whether black or white, silken gowns, low-cut shoes and hoods and stockings of various colours with other like fripperies of a luxurious nature.[19]

Wittesley reacted by threatening the wearers with greater excommunication if they did not put away such 'wanton finery' and return to their 'ancient and honourable mode of dress', giving them a month to comply. The bishop's letter indicates his dissatisfaction with the nuns in other areas besides dress, and so we now turn to look at how authority was exerted over the nunneries, who imposed it and the most common lapses from the monastic Rule.

V

Discipline and Authority

Nuns, whatever was intended, could never isolate themselves entirely from external authority either secular or spiritual. While they dealt mostly with religious authority, in Worcester represented by the local bishop or the prior of the cathedral, more remotely by the archbishop or even by the Pope and his officials, their cloistered life did not prevent the state regarding them as its subjects too, with the obligations this allegiance involved. The nuns must pay the king's taxes and obey his law, though from time to time their poverty gave them a special status.

As we have seen at their founding and in their early years, generous royal gifts such as wine and wood cheered and sustained the new nunneries. Also, Wroxall and Whiston both received annual grants from the Crown, originally by royal command. Wroxall's grant came only a few years after their founding. Whiston's was arranged in 1400, soon after Henry IV's accession. As a usurper king, perhaps the smallest charitable act might redeem his guilt and enhance his position with his subjects, and to this end he ordered the sheriff of Worcestershire to donate to the White Ladies £10 annually, out of the shire taxes.[1] There is repeated evidence of this grant's renewal and it was still being paid at the Dissolution in 1536. Sixty years before this, in 1476, the prioress, Margery Swinfen, no doubt to prove the nuns' continued gratitude, effusively promised the king, the Yorkist Edward IV, that she would hold four masses a year for the 'Solle of the noble prince of blessed memorie Richard Duke of York, father to our sayde soverayne lord' and another three masses for the king himself and the 'quene, my lorde prince, and there noble issue', and finally that every Friday her nuns would 'goo a procession saying the lateneye for the tranquylite and peas of the realme of England and remembrying our founder the Bishop of Worcester in the same'.[2]

51

Despite such royal favour the nuns were still liable for taxation, although it is unlikely that over the years their payments amounted to very much because, as we have seen, there are repeated references to their begging to be excused payment. The nuns could not so easily evade the law of the land. When Edward I imposed the Statute of Mortmain (1279) he intended to check the amount of land and other endowments religious houses received, because once such gifts became monastic property they were held in perpetuity and there was no opportunity for the taxation on death, paralleled by today's inheritance tax, that lay property owners had to pay. The statute laid down that a licence in mortmain must be bought before the nuns or any other corporation could legally hold the land. Mostly the nuns' donors appear to have complied with the statute; their gifts are recorded in the Patent Rolls as coming with a licence in mortmain. However, at Pinley in 1301, the nuns could show no such licence for a rent of corn and barley acquired from the late Peter de Montfort's estate. Consequently the prioress was only pardoned after she had paid a fine to the Exchequer.[3] This must have been an alarming experience for the small group of nuns, finding themselves the target of royal officialdom and then being forced to part with money they could ill afford to lose.

Professions

Not unexpectedly the nuns had a much closer and more regular relationship with religious authority than with the State. Profession days must have caused a buzz in the nunnery. Usually an episcopal official or another priest heard the novices' professions but occasionally the bishop or his suffragan came themselves. Bishop Reynold's register for 1309 leaves a record of 13 Wroxall nuns being professed before the suffragan bishop of Llandaff,[4] and Bishop Hemenhale, the diocesan, made a winter journey to Westwood in December 1337 to hear the professions there of 18 nuns.[5] This was a doubly unusual occasion: first in the large number of candidates and second that the local bishop, and not an official from Fontevrault, came to the convent for the occasion. It is doubtful that the 18 professees were all recent recruits. More likely, and as may have been the case at Wroxall, some of the women may have been patiently waiting several years to be officially professed, though meanwhile they would be considered tacitly professed and could thus have taken their full part in convent life. We do not know why the Bishop of Worcester took the service; he had no authority or place in the Fontevrault order. In theory the mother abbess in France should travel to hear the professions or, much more likely, one of her deputies. However, with the 1330s bringing the Hundred Years' War between England and France, the visit of a Frenchman to England may have been difficult and perhaps the prioress appealed to the local bishop for a remedy and he seized the chance to enter a door usually closed to him.

Some of the profession oaths survive. At Whiston in 1318, Sibilla de la Berewe vowed that:

I, sister Sibilla, promise stability of purpose and conversion of character and
obedience according to the rule of St Benedict, before God and his saints in
this monastery built in honour of the Blessed Virgin Mary.[6]

A more unusual oath was that sworn by Helena Ryons, the Gloucester girl
already mentioned. She used the same words as Sybilla but stipulated at the end that
she would not refrain from eating meat (*non sim arcata ab esu carnium abstinere*).[7] In
November of the same year the other Gloucester recruit, Margaret Fizeir, followed
her into the house, making her profession with the same caveat. One wonders what
story lies behind their unusual words. Perhaps they were delicate young women who
needed the extra food, or reluctant entrants who had bargained with their parents
and the nunnery over their terms of entry. Perhaps because they were both well-
born, the priores of Whiston, in the hope of generous entry dowries, was prepared
to make concessions. The two novices' spirit obviously impressed the monk writing
the Sede Vacante Register, for as he recorded their professions on the parchment he
sketched two wimpled faces in the margin, which are hardly faded today.

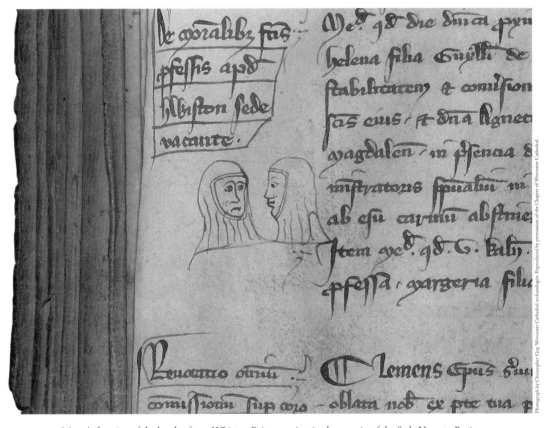

14   *A drawing of the heads of two Whiston Priory novices in the margin of the Sede Vacante Register.*

Choosing a Prioress

Elections must have caused another stir in the nunneries and further contact with the bishop or prior. A prioress could be elected by one of three methods. The most usual was by a unanimous vote of all the professed nuns, *per via spiritus sancti*, but if there were rival candidates, then votes had to be cast and counted and the result declared *per formam scrutini*. Alternatively, the bishop could bypass the nuns and make his own choice of a head for a house if he felt it either necessary or expedient to do so. Some of the best-preserved accounts of medieval prioresses' elections must be those of the diocese of Worcester. The Sede Vacante Register contains 17 documents recording the election of Alice Flagge as prioress of Whiston in 1308.[8] As Bishop Gainsborough had recently died the nuns, represented by Lucy de Solers, the sub-prioress, dealt with the cathedral prior and the bishop elect over the necessary procedures. Without a prioress they felt vulnerable and ill at ease, for no doubt they had heard tales of the Crown or bishops or powerful laymen laying hands on the revenues of leaderless nunneries. In fact, this was to happen at Wroxall in 1325 after the prioress's death when the escheator of Warwick, one John de Bolingbrok, seized the 'isues and profits' of the nunnery's lands. The outraged nuns must have appealed to the king, who came to their rescue and forbade the greedy John to 'intermeddle further' and to restore what he had already taken.[9] At Whiston the nuns moved fast enough in their vacancy to prevent any such mishap. The sub-prioress began by writing to Walter Reynolds, the bishop elect, pleading with him

15 *East wall of the White Ladies (Whiston) Priory church.*

for the licences necessary for the election and emphasising the physical want of her house, the 'poverty of their posssessions', which had previously driven them to begging in the streets of Worcester. Undoubtedly she was indicating that they had no money to pay any exorbitant fees or for prolonged negotiations. Fortunately the authorities were sympathetic and, despite the plethora of documents, the nuns were able to elect quickly, *via spiritus sancti*, Alice de Flagge as their new prioress, and she remained so for 20 years. As was customary, however, she at first refused the office, showing due Christian humility, but her sisters took no notice and the ritual was finally completed with the nuns singing a joyful Te Deum as they carried their new prioress to the church, she 'weeping, resisting as much as she could, and expostulating in a high voice as is the custom'.

Quite often the bishop exercised his right to choose and appoint his own candidate as prioress. This seemed to have happened when a nunnery suffered a crisis or was full of fractious quarrels and needed swift, firm action to right a situation and restore morale. At Wroxall, which was exceptionally troublesome in the 1320s and 1330s, Bishop Bransford appointed Isabel de Fockerham prioress in 1339 with 'the unanimous consent of the sub prioress and convent', stipulating sternly that 'the sisters of the house render due obedience to her' and that the recalcitrant would be restrained by 'ecclesiastical censure'.[10] Nevertheless, despite these words, he also declared that his intervention would not 'prejudice the nuns' rights to free election at future vacancies'. In the desperate years of the Black Death, in a different situation, Walter de Bransford again bypassed the nuns' rights by making his own appointments. Probably feeling he must act fast whenever a new leader was needed to maintain morale in a panicky situation, he appointed Matilda de Lyttlelton as prioress of the canonesses in Bristol in March 1349[11] and at Cookhill in May, although he had annulled the nuns' election of Christine Durvassal 'by scrutiny', he rapidly reappointed her on his own episcopal authority. At Whiston, too, he had to appoint a new prioress, as Prioress Juliana Power had died, most probably of the plague, which had carried off 11 of her nuns leaving only six to petition the bishop for a successor. In the 15th century the bishop continued to intervene in elections at Bristol, although the lords of Berkeley also maintained their ancient right to appoint the prioress. Thus in 1421 Bishop Philip Morgan, in what seems to have been a question of legal niceties, declared that the nuns' election of Joan Waleys was invalid but then went on to nominate her himself.[12] Yet when Joan Waleys died 34 years later, it was James, Lord of Berkeley who took control and granted the canonesses a licence to elect a new prioress.[13]

Clearly at Westwood the picture was once again different, for as with professions at this house neither the bishop nor the prior had rights over its appointments. Officially the abbess of Fontevrault chose the new prioress and in the 12th and 13th centuries the abbesses jealously guarded this privilege, resulting in major confrontations with their English houses. It has already been mentioned how the choice of prioress led to serious trouble at Nuneaton, and at Amesbury too the nuns wanted their own nominee rather than a foreign import. A letter survives from 1309 illustrating this. The writer is Princess Mary, sister of Edward II, who had lived at Amesbury since her early childhood. There she followed the religious life on her own terms and, despite an annual allowance of £100 spent on food and wine, fine horses and fires, she had still got into debt. However, she was obviously her monastic sisters' best choice to write a letter to her brother, the king, asking him to intervene with Fontevrault over the choosing of a new prioress. Her words so clearly evoke the situation that they are worth quoting at length:

> Very dear sire, as long time has passed since God did his will on our Prioress, we, after her death, sent in all haste to our dear cousin the Lady Abbess of Fontevrault, … asking for a lady from this our convent, to wit, for the Lady Isabella, whom we understand to be well able and sufficient for the office, that she might be granted to us for our prioress. And we thought dear sire, that she would have willingly granted us our request, … but as yet we have no answer and we understand from certain people that she intends to send us a prioress from beyond the sea there. And know certainly, my very dear brother, that should she send anyone other than one belonging to our convent, it would prove a matter of discord in the convent, and of destruction of goods, which I know well, sire, that you would not suffer willingly or wittingly, both for the love of me and our convent.[14]

Family rivalries may have been at work here as the abbess of Fontevrault was Eleanor of Brittany, Mary's cousin and a one-time nun of Amesbury who proved quite able to withstand both Edward's and Mary's demands, appointing her own candidate who must have had an uncertain welcome. Westwood does not appear to have been involved in any such dispute but as the 14th century wore on with the long hostility between France and England, everything French became more and more unpopular, and the power of Fontevrault over her English daughters appears to have diminished, while that of the authority of the local church increased. It would have been unwise of the English Fontevrault nunneries to remind people of their origins, especially when the Crown was targeting foreign religious houses, the alien monasteries, for heavy taxation or closing them completely. In church circles matters were made worse for these houses in that, during the Great Schism 1378 -1417 when there were two popes, one in France and one in Rome, England, still at war with France, naturally declared loyalty to the Italian Pope while the French and the order of Fontevrault supported his Avignonese rival. This division surfaced in the prioress's election at Westwood in 1384 when the Roman Pope, rather than the abbess at Fontevrault or the Avignonese Pope, instructed the prior of Worcester (there was a vacancy in see), to initiate the election process.[15] The former prioress had been loyal to Fontevrault and Pope Clement VII in Avignon, but obviously for this election the nuns would have to put forward a candidate supporting Rome if she was to be accepted by the prior. The first prioress chosen, Edith de Benacre, resigned within a year but Marie de Acton, the sub-prioress, her successor, whom the nuns chose *una voce et uno spiritu* (with one voice and spirit) subsequently led the house for the next 10 years. From this time, the late 14th century, there are other indications that the French allegiance was fading. In election documents of 1393 and 1405, although Fontevrault is mentioned, it is again the Worcester cathedral prior who is in charge of the election. Perhaps because of their historic links with the Angevin kings of England, the three Fontevrault nunneries in England escaped the penalties imposed on other alien priories, which all fell to a final closure in 1416. No doubt Marie de Acton and her successors, Eleanor Porter and Isabella Russell, were wise enough not to remind the authorities of their French history, especially when the war was in an active phase and anything French was detested and deeply suspect.

Visitations

Conscientious local bishops made frequent official visitations to their monastic houses. These must have been days of some anxiety to the nuns, since they were not primarily social or religious occasions but the medieval equivalent of a general inspection. On the chosen day, after the bishop and his retinue arrived and had been greeted at the gate by the prioress and her senior nuns, events would follow a well-established pattern. First in the church their father in God preached to the house, using a carefully selected text of which many are recorded, particularly from Godfrey Giffard's episcopate. In 1282, for instance, when visiting Whiston he preached on, '*Audi filia et vide et inclina aurem tuam*' ('Listen daughter and see, incline your ear'), a text also used at Pinley in 1284. In 1286 on Easter Eve, again at Whiston, which was so conveniently close to his cathedral, Giffard took appropriate words from Numbers: '*Letamini cras comeditis carnes*' ('Purify yourselves, tomorrow you will eat meat'), and some years later we know that at Pinley, Bishop Bransford preached on Micah 7:4, the rather obvious, '*Visitatio sua remit*' ('Your visitation comes'). But perhaps Bishop Montacute used the most double-edged words when he visited troublesome Wroxall in 1336 and chose for his homily, 'there was given to me a thorn in the flesh'.[16] Understandably bishops often used the same text several times, presumably giving the same sermon. Words from the Song of Solomon 1:3 were favourites of Godfrey Giffard, as was Ecclesiasticus 7:26, used at both Whiston and Cookhill in 1284. On lengthy visitation journeys such as Giffard's in January and February 1290, when he travelled through the diocese for several weeks on end, or Bransford's visitation in the late autumn of 1339, the bishop would visit every religious house worshipping, interviewing, advising, correcting and dining with the monks or nuns. To use a good sermon twice or more must have been a sensible way of easing the visitations' demands.

Whether it was a bishop or his commissary, after the service finished, the visitor interviewed each nun in turn, checking on her well-being, listening to any problems or complaints and no doubt admonishing or encouraging as necessary. He would complete the visit by eating with the community in the refectory or more likely, in the latter years, as the communal life fragmented, he might dine alone with the prioress and a few favoured nuns. If he came from a distance, the bishop and his following might also stay the night in the nunnery before continuing on their way the next day. Not long after his visit, if the bishop was not satisfied with what he had found and heard at the convent his written injunctions would arrive, as are recorded at Wroxall, or more generally they would receive Bishop Wittesley's injunctions for all the nuns of the diocese. These detailed the nuns' failings and how they were to be remedied. Altogether the visitations must have caused stress and upheaval for the nunnery. Often this may have been salutary, but for the impoverished houses the visit was also expensive as the priory would have to provide hospitality for the bishop and his retinue and also traditionally procurations, gifts of food, drink or money that they could often ill-afford to give. Some bishops were understanding enough to waive the procurations, as when Bishop Montacute went to Pinley in 1336 and Bishop Bransford to the same house in 1339.[17] In Bransford's register his clerk noted that his master did not dine with the nuns or stay the night. Instead he went on to nearby Rowington, a manor of the abbot of Reading, where most likely the bishop could be sure of a better meal and a more comfortable night's rest than at the indigent priory.

It is worth noting that when the see was vacant the cathedral prior took over the monastic visitations and he or his deputy were assiduous in their duties. Undoubtedly the prior had a financial motive: there were fees to be charged and a possible one-third share of a monastery's spiritualities to collect during a vacancy in see. But to spend a day with a house of nuns must also have been a welcome change from the all-male company of the cathedral priory. Certainly the prior's officer arrived swiftly at the Whiston gate in February 1339, only a few weeks after Bishop Hemenhale's death, and in 1419 on Bishop Thomas Peverell's death only 16 days intervened.[18] Yet though the prior may have welcomed the useful fees, he took his role as visitor seriously. At Wroxall Priory, probably in 1339, Robert de Clyfton, precentor of the cathedral church and prior's commissary, made every effort to straighten out their troubles, to correct the faults and slackness of the nuns and recall them to a true Benedictine Rule.

Forgetting the Rule

While they were by no means faultless, no major scandal appears to have touched the Worcester nuns. All misdemeanours seem to have been contained by the bishop or *in vacante* by the prior of Worcester, although from time to time rumours and gossip must have spread to the surrounding neighbourhoods since monastic houses were never entirely insulated from the secular world. Lay people, such as the corrodians and servants, lived on the site and others were frequently in and out of the enclosure. These facts alone led to problems as did the general weakening of the Rule, a situation mirrored throughout Christendom in the later Middle Ages, by a falling away from the ideal of an austere devotional life to one with little comforts and indulgences, abandoning of the communal life and forgetting the rule of silence.

Another rule of early monasticism was constantly broken. To St Benedict it was of prime importance that his monks and nuns must live in seclusion, for if they were to dedicate themselves wholly to the worship and service of God then the world with all its temptations and demands must not distract them. In 1298 Pope Boniface VIII made a strong attempt to recall all religious to a strict enclosure rule by issuing his decretal *Periculoso*, and in the Worcester diocese Bishop Giffard supported such a policy when he addressed a letter to all the nuns: 'That they do what is necessary for the inclusion and that they cause themselves to be enclosed this side the Gules of August'.[19] But such seclusion was difficult to enforce and it was understood, for example, that the prioress might need to ride out to visit the priory's granges or farms or visit one of the appropriated churches to check on how the appointed priest was faring. There are also instances recorded of nuns allowed out of the cloister to help with the harvesting of their fields, which must have been rough, hot work but a welcome change from their usual enclosed life. In Lincolnshire in 1440 the sub-prioress described how:

> in the autumn season the nuns go out to their autumn tasks, whereby the quire is not kept regularly, and … in seed time the nuns clear the weeds in the barns, and there the secular folks do come in and unbecoming words are uttered between them and the nuns.[20]

From this description it is obvious why bishops were worried by the nuns' disregard for enclosure. Despite all their strictures the women religious, and no doubt the men as well, continued to go out or persuaded their prioress to give them leave to join a pilgrimage or pay an occasional visit to their family or friends. Such customs were now too long established to make a return to the original Rule possible. That in practice they were now accepted as part of monastic life is clearly the case, as when in 1339 the sub-prior of Worcester, before a visitation, requested the Whiston nuns 'to summon any sisters who might be absent to be present'.[21] However, the nuns must have heard of the recent disaster that had overtaken Margaret Giffard, a nun from Shaftesbury, who, when travelling back to her nunnery after a visit to 'her earthly mother … in whose company she had lawfully been for some little time', had been 'seized and abducted' by 'certain henchmen of Satan … to the peril of their souls and the manifest prejudice of holy religion'.[22] The malefactors had then fled to the Worcester diocese where they might have remained at large. Obviously breaking enclosure, even if sanctioned, could open the way to worldliness or occasionally alarming danger. Sometimes poverty was used as an excuse to leave the nunnery, as when the Whiston nuns went out in the streets to beg or when at Cookhill Bishop Giffard instructed Thomas the chaplain to square up their affairs, adding that 'they are not to go out of the Cloister … nor wander about in the town'.[23] This was in 1285 but in the late 1330s authority was still struggling with the problem when the Worcester precentor commanded at Wroxall that 'the ladies' were not 'to go on foot to Coventry or Warwick as … they had hitherto done'.[24] Either the dazzle of the town must have been strong or the ladies hardy, or both, as these towns were several miles from the convent.

Not only the going out into but also the coming in of the world had to be disciplined. This had also been made clear in *Periculoso*, when Boniface VIII maintained that the coming in of seculars to the cloister was as much a danger to the consecrated life as the nuns venturing from their nunnery. Thus it is not surprising that on the same visit to Wroxall the precentor went on to demand that no layman was to eat in the frater, nor was any such one to be within the precincts at night time. At Pinley as well as Wroxall, it is clear such practices were common and Bishop Thoresby ordered 'the prioress and sisters' to remove 'certain seculars from their house within ten days, through whose presence they were being defamed'.[25] Fifteen years later the stern letter of Bishop Wittesley to all the women's houses shows that the situation had not improved, for, as well as castigating them over their dress, he also reprimanded them for frequenting the company of men and inviting seculars to their house where they indulged in 'lengthy conversations both by day and night'. It is easy to see why lay men and women were within the nunnery: the prioress would have to discuss business with her steward or she might also need to talk with the priory's tenants or those to whom she was bound through land or property. Then there were the corrodians, the lay boarders evident at Pinley and probably resident at the other houses too, who were in theory excluded from the nuns' inner enclosure but in smaller houses this area may not have been clearly defined. With no particular tasks to fulfil, they must have had plenty of time for talk with the nuns, gossiping of their lives in the world and telling spicy tales of places and people.

What really haunted the authorities was the fear of sexual impropriety. At Wroxall, far from the bishop's curia at Worcester, the nunnery in the 1320s and 1330s became an ungodly place where the nuns quarrelled, had no respect for their prioress and sat most lightly to the Rule. Bishop Montacute was to call it his 'thorn in the flesh', and earlier, in 1323, Bishop Cobham must have felt the same. The prioress, Agnes de Aylesbury, who appears as a weak woman with many faults, had lost control of the house, which had slid into serious disarray during her rule. One of the reasons that she had come to grief was her infatuation with a priest, John de Warton, on whom she had showered ill-afforded 'victuals and gifts' and, worse, he was her reputed partner in 'immoral relations'. Such a situation, whether it was true or not, was always the most serious of sins; it would bring the monastic life into scandalous disrepute and would take years to live down. Bishop Cobham dealt with this situation by forbidding the prioress any more dealings with de Warton, then he turned to the other problems he had found. First he had to deal with warring factions in the community: one was led by the prioress, the other by the Lady Isabella de Clinton, a well-connected widow and founder's kin. Their rivalry divided the house, 'the younger nuns siding with the prioress, the elder with the Lady Isabella'. Undoubtedly Agnes was an inadequate leader but Isabella, who had entered the house on her widowhood, played on her status to build up a coterie of critical, discontented nuns. The bishop had tried for sometime to amend affairs from a distance before visiting Wroxall to issue forthright injunctions. It was obvious that the prioress was no manager and had been selling off, 'the carpets, linen, goblets, saltcellars … intended for hospitable uses', thus 'the proper and customary hospitality and almsgiving have almost entirely ceased'. She had also neglected the building maintenance, bringing the priory to a 'ruinous condition'. The Lady Isabella for her part was making her chamber a centre for entertaining her friends and for a 'burdensome and unruly retinue' who disrupted the order of the house.[26] But despite the bishop's practical instructions to improve the situation, his ordering Lady Isabella to have a household 'chaste, peaceable and modest' and his requiring all the nuns to obey Agnes, the prioress soon gave up her office to be succeeded briefly by Isabella, the victorious incomer in the end. Sadly, quarrelling became a habit at Wroxall for some years; Bishop Montacute in his turn wearily complained of the problems the nunnery caused and his successor Bishop Bransford referred to 'recalcitrant nuns needing ecclesiastical censure',[27] while Robert de Clyfton, the cathedral precentor in his visitation (undated but probably 1339), found brawling and bad words to be the least of their sins.

The precentor determined to reform Wroxall Priory and as a priority he strove to recall the nuns to their Rule. Enclosure was to be strictly kept; there were to be no more visits to Warwick and Coventry. He ordered that 'all the doors of the cloister be locked at the sound of the curfew' and to prevent seculars coming in 'no layman in the night-time be within the door leading to the infirmary after curfew sounds'. He went on to command that in the church, the cloister, the frater and the dormitory the ladies were to keep silence and reminded them that they were a community and not individual groupings; thus at least two-thirds of convent were to eat together in the frater everyday. This last instruction was an attempt to deal with the now common practice of nunnery communities fragmenting into separate households where small groups of nuns gathered round a senior figure, such as the prioress or her deputy, sitting with her in her parlour, dining together in private and even abandoning the communal dorter for smaller bedrooms with their chosen circle. Interestingly, in the contemporary 14th-century poem *Piers the Plowman*, a similar situation appears in secular life. The poet complains:

> Elyng is the halle eche daye in the wyke
> Ther the lorde ne the lady liketh nougte to sytte
> Now hath vehe riche a reule to eten by hym-selve
> In a pryve parloure for a pore mennes sake,

16   *The entrance to the ruined refectory and cloister at Wroxall Priory.*

Or in a chambre with a chymneye and leve the chief halle
That was made for meles men to eten Inne'[28]

It seems that throughout society eating communally was, by the 1300s, considered uncivilised and old-fashioned: anyone up to date moved out of the noisy communal hall where the lord and his men all ate and drank together and instead dined in the quiet of a comfortable chamber with close family and one or two friends.

As well as Robert's anxiety to restore the monastic Rule, he also had great concern for the well-being and protection of an errant nun, Margaret Acton. She had been professed in 1307 so must have been near 50 at this time. It is not clear what her fault was but it could have been one of the worst, possibly apostasy, the sin of absconding from the convent perhaps out of homesickness or sheer unhappiness, or in the case of younger women to chase a dream of marriage and children. Obviously the precentor had felt at his visitation that Margaret was in danger of being victimised and bullied by the other nuns because he had punished her: 'none of you', he consequently wrote 'under pain of excommunication [are to] speak reproachfully or abusively' to her, and the prioress was now to watch for signs of contrition so that her penance could be alleviated and she was not to be deprived of her due 'sustenance and livelihood'.[29] Very likely poor Margaret Acton was being held in solitary confinement, which was the usual punishment for apostasy. She may also have been flogged, a customary humiliation for disobedient women religious as well as for the men. Frustratingly we hear no more of her, nor of the lady Alice de London of Pinley Priory, who was openly alleged to have apostatised in 1311.[30]

Apart from injunctions such as Bishop Wittlesey's to all the nuns of the diocese, no record of similar misbehaviour and reprimand remains for the White Ladies, Westwood, Cookhill or the Bristol canonesses. The White Ladies must have been physically too close to the bishop and prior and their officials for any major faults to go long unchecked. Certainly they seem to have retained the respect and affection of local people throughout their existence if legacies are any proof; if their lives had been openly scandalous surely this income would have dried up. One of the last donors to the house in the late 15th century is Hugh Oldebury; another is Thomas Partridge who, in 1470, left them half a mark, 3s. 4d., to pray for him.[31] A few years previously as already mentioned, a leading Worcester citizen, the dyer Robert Sutton and his wife, Johanna, had also left them money, 6s. 8d. and 5s. respectively. Compared with these gifts William Okeborne's legacy of 6d. to the Bristol house seems miserly, yet at that time (1455) it represented as much as three or four days' wages for a labourer.[32] At the Dissolution none of the houses incurred a condemnatory report. Indeed at Wroxall the nuns were 'all of good conversation and lyving', a far happier picture than that of 200 years before.

VI

The End

The idea of enforced closure was nothing new for English monastic houses. From time to time in the past, in varying circumstances, male monasteries and nunneries had closed or been shut down. Sometimes it might mean that one order took over the house of another; the monks or nuns of the first order moved out of the monastery and those of the other moved in. This had happened at Amesbury in 1177 when Henry II closed the old Saxon nunnery in order to refound it as a house of Fontevrault. Later, as we have seen, many alien priories were closed down but were often reopened as the new homes of native English houses. Such was the case in the early 15th century when the Crown took over the buildings of the expelled Fontevrault monks of Grovebury, soon to bestow them on newly founded Eton College and subsequently on the dean and canons of Windsor. However, a century later times had changed and Cardinal Wolsey's policy of closure was infinitely more drastic. Between 1524 and 1529 he closed 24 monastic houses, most of them indigent and small, some very small. A few, on the other hand, such as St Frideswide's in Oxford and Tonbridge Priory, both Augustinian houses, as well as the Praemonstratensian Bayham Abbey, were substantial communities. These three had reasonable incomes and more than a handful of occupants and, though at Tonbridge and Bayham local people strongly resisted closure, it was to no avail as Wolsey was determined on using the monastic revenues to found his Cardinal College at Oxford, for which he used St Frideswide's site. He intended it as a lasting testimony to his name but with his later disgrace it was soon renamed as Christ Church. In his planning Wolsey could claim good precedent as he must have known that only three years before in 1522, John Fisher, a devout and respected bishop of Rochester, had closed two nunneries, one at Broomhall in Berkshire and the other at Lillechurch in Kent, to provide for his new foundation, St John's College at Cambridge. Fisher could have claimed an even earlier precedent when Bishop Alcock of Ely, a former Bishop of Worcester, had closed St Radegund's nunnery in Cambridge in 1496 to found Jesus College. To divert the revenues of failing nunneries that were barely inhabited and in financial collapse for the support of fresh new institutions seemed a reasonable enterprise and this pattern was never entirely lost, even in the later wholesale destruction of the religious houses and chantries. Both Henry VIII and his son retained the cathedral monastery schools, which they refounded as the King's schools.

But in the mid-1530s the hope of financial gain undoubtedly drove Henry VIII's final campaign against the monasteries. By this time, through his own extravagance, through military adventures and through soaring inflation, Henry was desperately short of money. The monastic estates, with their widespread lands and property, their churches and libraries and with accumulated treasures, presented a tempting opportunity to redeem the situation. Moreover, the king suspected that many of the religious houses were still loyal to Rome, a loyalty that since 1534 was unlawful. All that was needed was an excuse to close down the monasteries and confiscate their assets to the Crown. The king and Thomas Cromwell, his newly appointed Vicar General, had only to devise a policy and to carry it forward with ruthless skill to achieve their aim.

As a first step, Henry had a survey made of the wealth of the whole English Church; this Valor Ecclesiasticus, drawn up in 1535, must have confirmed the king's resolve. The royal commissioners found the revenues of the monasteries to be immense. They had an income that could have been as much as £200,000 annually and added to this would be the capital value of the land and buildings and what lay within them. The royal revenues, in contrast, were as low as £100,000 a year. Therefore, almost at once, in the summer of 1535, Cromwell dispatched more commissioners to report on the condition of the smaller monasteries. These agents, led by Thomas Legh and Richard Layton, knew the agenda. That summer and autumn small groups of commissioners rode throughout the land, visiting all the small monasteries and nunneries to collect the evidence that would justify their closure – exaggerating in their reports any failing, though they could not condemn every house as slack or dissolute. Yet they gathered enough material for an Act to be presented to Parliament the next year, in which the preamble declared that because:

> Manifest sin, vicious, carnal and abominable living is daily used and committed among the little and small abbeys and priories and other religious houses[1]

these 'running sores' within the community were to be closed forthwith and their possessions surrendered to the Crown. An income of under £200 was made the benchmark of a smaller monastery and it caught the majority of houses. All the female houses of the Worcester diocese now faced their end. We have no first-hand knowledge of their reaction, though they must have felt as unhappy as the nuns of Legbourne Priory in Lincolnshire, who begged Cromwell to spare their house:

Please yt your goodnes to understonde that whereas almyghty God hath indued you with just title of Founder … to the great comfort of me and all my systers, we doo … submit oure selfes to youre most rightuouse commaundement and ordre … And wheras we doo here … that all abbyes and pryoryes under the value of cc ll be at oure moste noble prynces pleasure to subpresse and put downe, yet it may pleas your goodnes we trust in God ye shall here no complayntes agaynst us nother in oure lyvyng nor hospitalitie kepyng.[2]

They have 'noon othir comfort and refuge' but in Cromwell who, needless to say, did not spare them. Most of the Worcester nuns seem to have accepted their fate without official protest, though they too must have felt that they did not deserve closure. At Pinley, the commissioners had reported in 1536 that the four nuns and prioress, like their neighbours at Wroxall, were all 'of good conversation and living'.[3] At Bristol, too, the commission found no fault with the canonesses, though only two, the old prioress Eleanor Graunte and a novice, still remained in St Mary Magdalene's Priory. These two departed as June ended in the summer of 1536. Eleanor, who had years before been described as 'distinguished in every way by virtuous living and marked by grace' was now dismissed by the commissioners as 'impotent and aged'. Obviously her 16 years as prioress of an indigent and failing house had been hard and perhaps she was not sorry to abandon her responsibilities. However, despite it being such a poor house with goods only worth £21 11s. 3d., its 'juelles and plate' valued at £3 12s. 10d. and the lead and bells at 19s. 4d., she had not failed to keep the house 'in convenient reperation'.[4]

The expelled nuns had a choice for their future lives: they could either move to a larger remaining nunnery or they could apply for a 'capacity', which was permission to return to secular life. The Crown granted prioresses a taxable annual pension and sometimes pensions are recorded for nuns as well. Although the women must have been pleased with any recompense from the Crown, their pensions were far below those given to many monks. Jane Burghill, the last prioress of Whiston, had a pension of £5 10s. a year, which was still being paid in 1553; the prioress of Westwood, on the other hand, did better, gaining £10 a year. Prioress Agnes Lyttle of Wroxall was awarded £7 10s., though Margaret Wygston of Pinley had to manage on an annual £4.[5] With a singular lack of generosity, the government imposed a 10 per cent tax on these sums so that their modest value was reduced even further. One nun at Pinley asked for a capacity but the five nuns at Wroxall 'desyr all, yf the howse be suppressed, to be sent to other religious howses'. No grants are recorded for the nuns at Whiston so they probably all went on to other nunneries. The single novice nun at Bristol is recorded as 'desiring continuance in religion'.[6] But five nuns at Westwood had had enough of monastic life and each took away 'rewards' totalling £6 1s. 8d. as they left their erstwhile home to return to the world.[7]

At Cookhill the story was surprisingly different. Despite its history of powerlessness and poverty, Cookhill managed to evade dissolution in 1536. It could not possibly have pleaded an income of over £200 a year so why was it spared? The answer lies within the Letters and Papers of Henry VIII: quite simply, the nuns of Cookhill had a friend at court. In 1542 the Letters and Papers record that Thomas Brook, a wealthy London merchant tailor, gave up a 99-year lease granted to him by the nuns of Cookhill in 1537 'in consideration that by his labour the said nunnery was saved from suppression.'[8] In the short term he appears to have averted Cookhill's closure probably because the king was his debtor since, as the same source also records, Brook and several other wealthy men had agreed in 1536 that they were 'contented to forbear unto a longer day' the king's repayment of debts to them.[9] But even the intervention of a confident patron could not prevent the inevitable end for Cookhill. In either 1539 or the year before, the house closed and the prioress, Elizabeth Hughes, and her six nuns dispersed. Yet the delay had gained them one advantage: by 1538 Henry's campaign against the monasteries had moved on and now all the remaining houses were being forced to close. Thus, since the earlier option for the displaced religious to join another house was no longer available, they all had to be given a money payment, and so at Cookhill in 1540 the Crown granted not only the prioress but also all the nuns a pension, the amounts carefully reflecting the monastic hierarchy. Five nuns, Joan Bellamy, Alice Wastle, Margery Dyson, Anne Reve and Elyn Owley each received 53s. 3d. a year; Anne Morgan, the sub-prioress, gained 56s. 8d. and the prioress, Elizabeth Hughes, only appointed in 1537, topped the list with £8 annually.[10]

There has been debate among monastic historians about how the pensions of ex-religious were calculated. What were the criteria for settling their amount? Looking at the Worcester nunneries the value of the prioresses' pensions correlates with the value of the annual income of their house at the Dissolution; that is the higher the monastic income, the higher the prioress's pension, and this formula seems the same for the men. Thus while the abbot of wealthy Evesham Abbey – income a massive £1,183 12s. 9d. a year – gained a commensurate pension of £240 per annum, the prior of Little Malvern, whose house's income was a mere £98 10s. 9d., was granted only £11 13s. 4d. Similarly, for the women at Westwood, which had the highest income of the Worcester nunneries at £75 19s. 11d., its last prioress gained the highest pension of £10. The only exception to this scale was Cookhill, where the prioress's £8 pension was second only to Westwood, yet the priory came fourth in the value table, with less than half of Westwood's income. Thomas Brook's influence at court might explain this anomaly. Perhaps he agreed to withdraw his opposition to Cookhill's closure if the Crown awarded the prioress and her house reasonable pensions. What is more certain is that the commissioners must have used some subjective judgement in setting the pension levels. If not, why did Jocosa Acton of Westwood gain £10 a year while Prioress Anne Lyttle of Wroxall received only £7 10s., when the difference in annual value of their houses was a only £8? Westwood may have reminded the visitors of its ancient royal connections, or there may have been special pleading by Robert Acton, one of the Valor commissioners, on behalf of his putative kinswoman, Prioress

Jocosa Acton. Robert Acton had much to do with the ending of the monasteries. As sheriff of Worcestershire, he was well placed to feather his nest when lands and other property became available. He was on hand when Hailes Abbey closed and his rapacity obviously shocked a forthright servant, who reported that she had seen a night-time visitor bringing him locks from the abbey and she had chided him with, 'Alas, why do you receive this stuff?' to which he replied, 'Hold thy peace, for it is there now catch that may catch.'[11] Acton would have had no guilt about his actions; he was only one of many benefiting from the situation and, by 1539, he was already enjoying the profits of his new lands from the Westwood Priory estate.

Apart from four of the prioresses, the nuns of Worcester diocese now disappear from recorded history. We can, however, make some reasonable speculation about their subsequent lives. The majority probably returned to their homes. Jane Burghill may have ridden back to Herefordshire, where the Burghills were a well-known family. They probably originated from the village of Burghill, not far from Hereford, and by the 16th century they were obviously prospering – they are known to have held one of the two manors at Thinghill, three or four miles from the city, while at Hereford Cathedral one William Burghill was treasurer from 1519-26. Jane's worthwhile pension may have eased a return to this family, though there is no trace of her or any subsequent history in local Hereford records. The younger nuns may have married and others may have established small shared households, where they quietly continued in a religious life, not wearing a habit but faithfully saying the offices together until death dispersed them. There is researched evidence of such outcomes for former nuns elsewhere. David Knowles, for example, maintains that by the 1550s nearly 30 per cent of the Lincolnshire nuns had married once Edward VI's government had repealed the Six Articles Act of 1539, which had forbidden the marriage of ex-religious. For although Henry VIII had destroyed their lives and had made impossible the rules of poverty and obedience, he had unreasonably refused to free former monks and nuns from their vow of chastity. Despite Knowles's research, others doubt his view that generally many former nuns married; Marilyn Oliva could find no record of such marriages in Norwich diocese, in Yorkshire a tiny fraction, only six out of 216 ex-nuns, seem to have married and in London only two marriages can be traced.[12] Ironically though, Prioress Joan Missenden, who had pleaded so pathetically that Legbourne Priory should continue, once free took advantage of her new circumstance and soon became Mrs Otley of Corby in south Lincolnshire.[13] Perhaps she knew that the prioresses of Gokewell and Ankerwyke, two other Lincolnshire nunneries, had followed the same path, as well, as half the nuns at Sixhill.[14] But generally it is difficult to follow the nuns in their post-Dissolution lives. Whereas many of the former monks took up posts as parish priests and chaplains and appear in the appropriate documents, for the women only the occasional will or property lease gives any further clue to their subsequent lives.

It was probably the older ex-nuns who found it most testing to give up the community life, a way some of them had lived for decades. The Cookhill nuns would soon have heard that Dame Elizabeth Throckmorton, the last prioress of Denny Abbey near Cambridge, had returned to her family home at Coughton Court and was living there with two of her former nuns. Coughton was no distance from Cookhill and the nuns there must have known of this continuing monastic household. There are similar instances in the dioceses of York, Norwich and Lincoln and in the West Country of other small continuing communities. Very likely, therefore, of Worcester's nuns at the Dissolution, a few may have gone on living in community together. The identity of some of the new owners or tenants of the monastic lands encourages this idea and makes it possible that some of the nuns could even have remained in a corner of their old buildings, or in the home farm, or in some other previously monastic property. For example, in another diocese, two former nuns of Shaftesbury Abbey, Margaret Mayo and Edith Maudlen, were still living in small dwellings within their old monastic precinct in the 1560s.[15] In Worcester diocese new occupiers of several of the monastic sites share the same name as former prioresses. At Whiston, where Margery Welshe had been the penultimate prioress, Walter Welshe gained a lease on the priory buildings; at Westwood, as we have seen, Robert Acton gained a considerable share of the lands, mostly distant or outlying but including the manor and church at Crutch, almost adjacent to Westwood and from the beginning one of the monastic possessions. Crutch may have become a home for some of the Westwood nuns while they recovered from the shock of their eviction. Finally at Pinley, where Margaret Wigston was the last head, one William Wigston paid the Crown £342 11s. in 1544 for the site and the demesne lands.[16] This coincidence of names must have some significance; at the Dissolution, at half the Worcester women's houses, new occupiers of the monastic land appear to be related to a former prioress. A similar pattern is found elsewhere as J.H. Bettey's study of the dissolution of the West Country monasteries shows. Giving the reason that 'as uncertainties over the future grew', he lists many religious houses where, from the early 16th century, relatives of the abbey heads gained leases on monastic land or acted as bailiffs or stewards of the estates.[17] It seems that those who foresaw closure and knew the worth of the monastic estates were quick to forestall the Crown by closing in and acquiring a share. Whether or not in Worcester they then allowed a home to any of the former nuns we may never know.

Not only did the religious suffer homelessness but the nuns' servants must also have faced an uncertain future. The domestic servants, those who worked for the nunnery household, would have been most at risk. At Pinley, for example, there were three hinds and four female servants as well as a woman corrodian. At Wroxall there were 10 servants – seven hinds and three dairy maids – and even tiny Bristol housed a man of all work and a laundress.[18] The priories also employed shepherds and cowmen, ploughmen and woodmen as well as using skilled craftsmen such as the thatchers and carpenters and plasterers who all appear in the Westwood accounts. Now they faced unemployment but, hopefully, anyone taking on the wider estate would retain the outside workers; it was the household workers who were no longer needed. Very likely the nuns, as they left their priories, took some of the servants with them, employing them in their new homes or finding them a niche within their families. At Westwood the commissioners showed some compassion, not only giving the nuns rewards but also the servants: they gained £1 6s. 8d. each as a one-off reward and then, including the vicar of Cotheridge, were also paid a total of £7 0s. 6d. in wages. Again at Westwood, old Elizabeth Mounteford, already mentioned, who may have been a corrodian, took away £2 0s. 8d.[19] Hopefully similar arrangements were made for the other corrodians such as the one at Pinley, who may well have been too old and too vulnerable to be unexpectedly homeless without financial support.

One group of religious who suffered no trauma at the Dissolution were the monks, the canons, at Westwood. They had disappeared from sight by the early 15th century. It is probable that as the Hundred Years' War dragged on in the century before, the Fontevrault houses in England became more and more wary of their French connection. The government were not treating such alien houses well: they were having to pay high taxes and some were closed. Others thought it wise to sever their foreign links and take denizen status. By doing this on payment of a substantial fee, they became English houses. We know that Amesbury became denizen after

17   *Westwood House, a late 16th-century building.*

1403 and Nuneaton about 1412 and, although there is no record, Westwood must have taken the same path at about the same time. Strangely, the prior of Worcester did not list the nunnery as alien in his return of such houses in 1374,[20] nor did the prioress attempt to disguise the nunnery's origins when, in an election return of 1405, the priory was still described as of Fontevrault.[21] The timing of the disappearance of the male element from the English Fontevrault houses parallels that of lay brothers resident in male Cistercian and Benedictine houses. With the drop in population brought by the Black Death and the subsequent demand for labour coupled with urban growth, there would be more opportunities for males to make a living in town or countryside than retreating to a monastery. However it was, in all three Fontevrault houses records of the priors and canons ended at this time. We find final references at Nuneaton and Amesbury in 1424 and 1403 respectively and at Westwood Prior William, mentioned in 1371, may be the last of a line that began at the nunnery's founding. Thus by the time of the upheaval of the 1530s the male religious at Westwood had been gone for more than 100 years.

The new owners, who were largely local men, may have looked considerately on the monastic employees. They came from the landowning gentry and would be ambitious to add to their existing estates. At Westwood John Pakington, lord of nearby Hampton Lovett and with Robert Acton one of the Valor examiners of the nunnery, took over much of the priory estate. He pleaded that as 'I am now in the king's service in north Wales to my great charge', he needed more land, not only to increase his income, but also to provide grass for the mounts necessary to his arduous office with the lengthy travelling involved.[22] The Pakingtons remained at Westwood, living in the Elizabethan mansion they built until the last years of the 19th century. At Whiston in 1543 the king granted Richard Callowhill, a prominent local clothier, the priory site and much of the local land was still leased to Walter Welshe, while lands at White Ladies Aston and elsewhere had already gone to Thomas Hill and his son, William.[23] By the early 17th century the Six Masters Charity, which supported Worcester's ancient grammar school, had taken on the Whiston site and three centuries later, in 1868, the Royal Grammar School moved from the crowded city centre to its present spacious home. It was a little different at Cookhill where in 1542 an apparent outsider, Nicholas Fortescue, gained the priory site and lands. Fortescue is variously described as 'grome porter' of the Court (Leland) or 'Chamberlain of the Exchequer' (Prattinton) and the grant was made to him and his wife Katherine. They and their descendants lived at Cookhill until the early 19th century when the male line died out. At Bristol the Dissolution commissioner Richard Ryche wrote to Cromwell that he had let the site 'to Wykes at the desire of Mr Controller',[24] but this appears a short-term arrangement as in 1545 Henry Brayne, a London merchant tailor, bought the priory site and most of its land and property, including 20 houses in Bristol, from the Crown.[25] At £17 8s. 10d. he must have felt he had a bargain, since he had had to give nearly 40 times as much, £667 7s. 6d., for nearby St James Priory, his other local purchase. Like his predecessor, Brayne's occupation of the nunnery

71

site was short lived. Obviously he had only seen it as a property speculation, for in 1554 he sold it on to a local man from north Somerset, William Gorges, whose father was already the tenant.[26] By now it was called 'the Mawdeleyns' and became the Gorges' home until the end of the century.

In Warwickshire the closure of Wroxall and Pinley seems to have proceeded smoothly. In character with their 'good conversation and lyvyng' all the nuns left for their new lives[27] and, as has already been suggested, the Wygston family, who were much involved in the final days of Pinley Priory's life, may have eased the transition of the last prioress, their probable kinswoman Margaret, into the secular world. The Valor Ecclesiasticus records one Roger Wygston as the priory's steward, retained at 20s. a year. Another or the same Roger Wygston was one of the visiting Valor commissioners and at Pinley's dissolution Roger Wygston gained the grain, chattels and ornaments of the nuns while the Crown granted his son, John, the lease of the priory. Later, John surrendered the lease to his elder brother, William, who finally bought the priory site from the Crown for £342 11s. in 1544.[28] When William in his turn leased out part of his new land in 1547, the church and cloisters were already in ruin, with the church being used as a shelter for sheep.[29] Many years later in 1599, a very old lady, one Margaret Watnoll aged 95, remembered that local people had once attended the ruined church where 'they did marrye, burye and christen'.[30] It was now lost irretrievably to the community. Both William Wygston and his father appear as powerful local figures, since both were in turn sheriffs of Warwickshire as well as Justices of the Peace. They are typical of the up-and-coming gentry class who gained so widely from the dispersal of the monastic lands. Another Valor Ecclesiasticus commissioner who benefited from his preview of the monastic land was Robert Burgoyne. He with John Scudamore, also a commissioner, paid the king £588 12s. 4d. for Wroxall in 1544.[31] Their prize included the buildings and all the monastic site, the gardens, orchards and fishing of the Wroxall pool as well as the rectory and tithes of Wroxall. Soon Scudamore, who had recently acquired Dore Abbey in Herefordshire as well, gave up his share to the Burgoynes, possibly on Robert's death the next year when another Robert, his son, inherited it. The first Robert Burgoyne was the younger son of John Burgoyne of Sutton in Bedfordshire and he must have seized the chance to gain an estate for himself, an opportunity usually denied by primogeniture. The Burgoynes remained at Wroxall for 170 years and then sold out to another man anxious to achieve the status of country gentleman – he was England's greatest architect, Sir Christopher Wren.

As the nunneries went into lay ownership the nuns themselves disappear into the secular world. The Court of Augmentations pension list for 1553 records Prioress Anne (or Agnes) Lyttle of Wroxall as still receiving her pension, as was Jane Burghill of Whiston, already mentioned.[32] As well as the pension payment record, two most interesting and relevant wills still survive. The first is Joyce Acton's, 'sometime prioress of Westwoode', made in December 1564 when she was 'sycke in body' and close to death.[33] She died within a month and was buried on a winter day,

18
Fifteenth-century doorway in the barn of Pinley Priory, formerly the nuns' church.

11 January 1565, in the churchyard of All Saints Worcester, near the river Severn. Most valuably, the church register tells us something further about her since the clerk recording her burial wrote after her name 'vestalis', meaning 'a nun'. Obviously in the nearly 30 years since Westwood closed, Jocosa had continued to live some sort of religious life, dwelling at her death somewhere in All Saints parish in the city of Worcester. Others may have joined her but no evidence for this can be found. In her will the prioress left all her property to Robert Hollins, who was to be her sole executor, apart from 10s. to 'all hallows church to by a Bible'. It seems that Jocosa Acton, by this latter gift, despite her apparent loyalty to her past, had conformed to the Protestant ethos of the reformed Church in England. Other wills of this time still bequeath money for lights (candles) in the church and other Catholic customs,

yet she did none of this, providing a Bible instead, presumably the English version, which by law every church now had to have. Bibles were an expensive item and undoubtedly the priest and wardens of All Hallows must have been grateful for the prioress's bequest. The other will, that of an Elizabeth Huwes, is a less certain proposition. Nowhere in the document is Cookhill Priory mentioned but it seems likely that the Elizabeth Huwes making this will in 1558, 20 years after Cookhill's end when Elizabeth Hughes was named as the last prioress, was once that priory's head. In the tradition of the old religion she bequeathed her soul to God and 'Our Lady Saint Mary and to all the blessed saints of heaven' and her body to be buried in the chancel of Spernall church. Spernall was long associated with Cookhill Priory and a burial in any chancel was always a sign of status and thus a fitting resting place for a one-time prioress. Elizabeth went on to bequeath to Spernall church a vestment of Nantes cloth – did it come from the priory? – and also a 'towell', obviously earmarked for liturgical use. Then, after many bequests of sheep, cows and calves to her brother, her nephews and nieces and her godchildren and servants, she gave her black mare to the parson of Spernall.[34] The inventory appended to the will completes the picture of an unmarried woman of some substance, to whom the church and its life were important; the Elizabeth Huwes of this 1558 will fits well into a former prioress's frame. Maybe, as she had only held office for the priory's last year, she had soon slipped off that persona or maybe she felt it unwise to mention it in the religious uncertainty of late 1558.

The post-Dissolution lives of these prioresses and the nuns of their houses may have brought new freedoms and opportunities but there must have been much sadness too, particularly when they saw the ruin of their convent homes. One witness is John Leland, who travelled the whole of England between 1534 and 1543 visiting every 'bay, river, lake, mountain, valley, moor, heath, wood, city, castle, manor house, monastery and college' in the land – in fact his intensive travel and assiduous recording became too much for him and he died insane in 1552. In Worcester he describes 'Whitestan' as once 'a Place of Nunnes, the Church cleane rased downe and a Farme Place in the Residew of the Buildings'.[35] Such a scene must have been constantly replicated on the old monastic sites. Time, social customs, religious thought and practice had moved on: in England, the priories and abbeys became part of history, their buildings relics of a bygone era.

VII

Remnants and Ruins

What remains? What is left of Worcester's medieval nunneries? In fact, quite a lot can be seen of the buildings, and artefacts and documents can also be uncovered. This is surprising in the sense that nowadays the existence of the nunneries is little known and considering that none of the houses were great buildings with lavish furnishings or ornamentation.

Westwood

Ironically, it is the most prestigious house of which no physical trace remains. Not even the exact site of Westwood Priory is known today. It lay somewhere in the spacious park that surrounds Westwood House. This house is often assumed to have been built where the nunnery once stood. John Pakington, Queen Elizabeth I's favoured 'Lusty' Pakington and the first John Pakington's great nephew, began to build the house in the late 16th century. He embarked on a substantial hunting lodge of Tudor brick that his successors soon developed into a lofty mansion, but its vaulted cellars could date to before Lusty's time and the kitchen garden, in the past, has turned up old building stones. On the other hand, there is a family tradition that Lusty Pakington, out of respect for the nuns and their holy lives, did not disturb the monastic remains and chose a new location for his great enterprise. An alternative position for the nunnery lies on the southern slope of Nunnery Wood, some distance to the north-west of Westwood House. Thomas Habington, writing in the early 17th century, described the priory as set 'in a vast and solitary wood' where 'religious women who, retyred from the world, were devoted to God', and he goes on to say that 'the nunnery was somewhat distant from thys house and differing in situation'.[1] In this context Habington could be a reliable witness, for he was born about 1560 and in his youth he must have met local people with a living memory of

Photograph by Johnnie Pakington.

19 *Portrait of Sir John Pakington, great nephew and namesake of the first owner of the Westwood Estate. A favourite of Elizabeth I, he built the Westwood mansion.*

Westwood Priory and its location. At the bottom of the wooded slope in Westwood Park are pools, which could well be the successors of the monastic fishponds, and not far from them a stone-lined well. Higher up the slope in the wood, a medieval stone coffin and its broken lid, with the interior shaped to surround a human body, lay for many years; today it is in the County Museum at Hartlebury Castle. There are also well-founded reports of other evidence found at this site, of eight other coffins, bones gathered up and reburied and ancient tiles, all of which might indicate the monastic cemetery and traces of domestic or religious buildings. In the early 19th century Philip Prattinton, the Worcester antiquarian, wrote of another stone fragment. It had been found 'many years ago in cleaning a pond in Westwood Park' and it read in part:

20   *Westwood House gateway.*

'(L)ECORS ... MABLE ... GYST ... CI ... IHU ... DE ... SA ... ALLME
... HA ... MERCI+'[2]

Despite the uncertainty of the inscription, it seems safe to say this fragment
must have been part of another coffin lid or some sort of memorial stone. None of
this evidence makes the location of the nunnery definite but it seems most likely

21   *Stone coffin and part of a cover found in Westwood Nunnery Wood, a possible site of the nuns' priory.*

that it lay in the lower area of Nunnery Wood, still within the park, rather than on the site of Westwood House. Only a full-scale excavation could provide an answer. Wherever the nunnery lay and whatever their regard for it, the Pakingtons obviously let the buildings collapse into ruin, as was the government's goal, yet by careful intent or by great good fortune, they preserved for over 350 years several hundred medieval documents, which provide the best monastic archive of all the female houses in the medieval Worcester diocese. Today the collection, known as the Hampton Papers, is to be found in Worcester Record Office.

Whiston

Evidence for the locations of all the other houses, however, still exists either in building remains or documentary accounts. At Whiston, Cookhill, Wroxall and Pinley something can be seen of each monastic church and a little of the priory buildings. Post-Reformation evidence also indicates the disposition of other vanished parts of the nunneries. At Whiston, the Six Masters records tell of the demolition of some of the monastic buildings, with wood and nails being removed from the site to be sold or used elsewhere, and we know that even in the Callowhills' time building timber was being sold off, as in 1554 timbers from the White Ladies were used for the repair or rebuilding of the Queen Elizabeth House in the city. Yet on the site today, home of the Worcester Royal Grammar and Alice Ottley School, not everything has gone. The east and west walls of the nuns' church remain, as do the lower courses of the other two walls, so it is easy to see the exact size of the area enclosed by the church, which is set out as an attractive garden. The east wall is built into the White Ladies house and at the west end two blocked-up doorways are evident, one of which was probably an entrance towards the Tything for townsfolk to enter the church. The other, according to the 1848 Archaeological Association Report, led to the famed 'secret passage' to the cathedral.[3] It is much more likely that a barrel-roofed deep drain or water conduit, leading from or to the nunnery site, gave this mistaken impression. Such a passage, 'five or six feet deep, and arched over with stone', was broken into under the High Street in the early 19th century when water pipes were laid. And earlier ''tis said', Dr Nash, the local antiquarian and historian, intrepidly entered the passage from the White Ladies end 'until his torch going out he gave up his subterraneous researches'.[4] Today the passage is blocked with rubble and the entry sealed. Below the church was a crypt, which is depicted in a print of 1830 as a simple unadorned space with low arches to support the church above.[5] In 1848 the British Archaeological Association visited Worcester for their annual congress, making the White Ladies site one of the main foci of their afternoon excursions. They thoroughly investigated the crypt but reported the central arch as broken down. When they moved outside the church, however, their activities proved more exciting. The visitors had a trench dug on the south side and this yielded a stone coffin and several skeletons, which they conjectured

22 *Nineteenth-century drawing of the crypt of the White Ladies nunnery church, showing entrance to the 'secret passage' at the far end.*

might have been those of the prioresses. Ten years later most of the vaulting and the roof of the crypt had collapsed and only one arch remained over the wood store at the west end. Today the whole crypt is lost. To the north of the church, in 1959, more skeletons were unearthed when workmen were preparing for a new school building. These bones must indicate the site of the monastic cemetery, which was often placed to the north or north-east of the church, and a tile lying among the remains dates the burials to the 15th century. Early 19th-century plans of the Six Masters Charity also show fish ponds beyond the cemetery and a tithe barn lying along the Tything.[6] The core of the monastic buildings probably lay to the south of the church – a refectory is mentioned in local histories and journals. For example, Valentine Green in 1796 wrote that, 'the refectory remains in its primitive state, a spacious and handsome apartment' though 'the chapel was ruined on the dispersal of the nuns.' He also trod 'the nuns' walk' in the garden.[7]

Regarding artefacts, apart from the tile and pottery finds, nothing definite survives. A portrait reputed to be that of Jane Burghill, the last prioress, was stolen from the Commandery Museum in the city some years ago and the only other possible relic is a small and precious alabaster sculpture kept in Worcester Cathedral. It is thought to have once belonged to the Whiston nunnery but there is no documentary evidence to verify such a claim. The sculpted Virgin forms the centrepiece of a triptych, with two painted panels either side. These are original, as are the traces of paint on the carved figures of Mary carrying her Child, which are the work of the well-known Nottingham school of alabaster sculpture, and they probably date to the reign of Edward IV (1460-85).

Photograph by Christopher Guy, Worcester Cathedral Archaeologist. Reproduced by permission of the Chapter of Worcester Cathedral.

23 *The Virgin and Child, 15th-century alabaster, reputed to have belonged to Whiston Priory.*

Cookhill

At Cookhill, on the other hand, there is no doubt about the ownership of another bas relief of the Virgin, this time crowned in glory. Again sculpted in alabaster, it stood in a niche in the blocked east window of the nunnery church until 1936, when it was moved to the Birmingham Museum and Art Gallery where it was on public display. The maker was one of the prolific Nottingham school, chiefly working in the 14th and 15th centuries. The relief cannot be precisely dated as there is no maker's mark, but it is probably of the 15th century. Painted in gold and gaudy primary colours, it depicts the Virgin crowned in glory with a golden crown upon her head and wearing a blue mantle. The halo is red and a mandorla of gold

24 *Relief of the crowned Virgin from Cookhill Priory.*

Photograph by Christopher Guy, Worcester Cathedral Archaeologist. Reproduced by permission of the Chapter of Worcester Cathedral.

rays surrounds the whole figure. Beyond the mandorla are supporting angels, four on each side, with alternating blue and gold wings and at the bottom of the relief are two kneeling figures, one perhaps the donor and the other thought to be St Thomas. From the St Thomas figure a scroll runs up to the Virgin, probably intended to carry a prayer. Altogether the relief, though somewhat damaged and worn, is an interesting example of late medieval popular art. It is not of the finest quality but must have been much prized by the nuns when the donor presented it to their nunnery. It is almost certainly part of a much larger altar reredos, where it could have been the central panel of a life of the Virgin with two or three further scenes on either side, or alternatively it may have been a side panel of another reredos with the Crucifixion taking the centre space. If there were ever further panels at Cookhill, they are not to be found.

The Cookhill chapel itself has lost all its glory and until recently it has been a store with little sign of its ancient purpose. Only a part of the medieval walls remains, the north wall has two original windows and in the east the window is blocked; the rest of the chapel is largely brick built and all the ecclesiastical furnishings still shown in the VCH illustration of the late 19th century have gone.[8] But today the building is in better condition than in the picture in Nash's *Worcestershire*, where the sketch of 1781 shows a roofless ruin with tumbled walls.[9] It must have been not long after that when Captain John Fortescue undertook the restoration, rebuilding the walls in brick and surrounding the new roof with a stylish and fashionable 'gothic' crenellation. He placed the alabaster Virgin in a niche in the blocked east

25   *Cookhill Priory church, substantially rebuilt in the early 19th century.*

window and retained a medieval piscina in the outside of the north wall. Although the captain probably swept away precious medieval fragments from the chapel, he must have saved the mainpart by his making the building watertight. He made the chapel a shrine to his Fortescue forebears; many were buried in the subterranean vault and memorials to family members adorned the walls or paved the floor. The foundress, Isabella de Beauchamp's, tomb may have disappeared at this time as there is no further record of it.

Little else remains of the nunnery, though very likely the brick and timber building range at the back of the house could be a late monastic structure, and a hundred years ago there were worked broken stones in the garden walls, which may have come from the chapel but are now all so weathered that it is difficult to pick them out. However, fishermen still fish the ponds in front of the house, which must be a part of the priory's water system, while the VCH describes them as a moat and points to two depressions as the medieval stew ponds.[10] Away from the site the British Museum holds a seal of the convent and, more excitingly, only a

26 *Cookhill Seal matrix, showing the Virgin and Child with a kneeling figure.*

few years ago, in 1989, the matrix of the prioress's seal was found in a nearby field. It depicts the Virgin and Child seated and around the edge is inscribed in Latin, 'the seal of the Prioress of Cookhill'. From its worn state it looks as if it was used for many years and must have been a tiresome loss for the nunnery if it disappeared while still in use. It could date to the 13th century and is kept by the Worcester County Museum.

Wroxall

At the Warwickshire sites clear evidence survives of the nuns' lives. If Sir Christopher Wren ever came to his gentleman's residence, he would have found at least part of the church and ruined buildings on the east and south sides of a small cloister. On the fourth side, the west, the Burgoynes had built their house and in this Sir Christopher's descendants made their home. But it has gone today for, in 1876, the last of the Wrens sold the estate to a Liverpool magnate, who pulled down the old house to make way for a far grander home. Fortunately James Dugdale chose to build away from the monastic site, which he dwarfed with his huge red brick mansion that still dominates the parkland and gardens around it. Traditionally, it is said that Wren added the curious brick tower to the church but Pevsner dated it to 1663-4, more than 40 years before Wren purchased the estate; thus it cannot be Sir Christopher's

design. The church is largely built of stone and dates from the early 14th century when we know that after alteration it was reconsecrated, but the small church of today is considered to be only a part, the north aisle, of the original building, of which the rest has disappeared. Inside are monuments to the Wrens and some good late medieval glass as well as a brass of about 1430. To the south of the church lie the broken walls of the monastery. It is possible to pick out a rectangular chapterhouse on the east side of the vanished cloister, distinguished by the quality of some of the crumbling, fragmentary stonework. Pevsner considered that it could have seated 10 but it is certainly not large. In the south range, what was once the refectory and perhaps a warming room can be made out with low doorways in between. The small complex of buildings, now ruined and uncared for, was never on a large scale but probably designed to suit a community of 12 or so nuns, even though the chapterhouse could not hold them all. Somewhere beyond the cloister further, less substantial buildings would have housed the servants and provided for baking and brewing and storage of food supplies. At the edge of today's gardens, to the south-west where the ground drops away to give a fine wide view, there is a pool that could well indicate the monastic stew ponds and is evidence of the priory's water supply. Having been a girls' school until the 1990s, the house is now a country mansion hotel with the nuns' church as a wedding venue, a strange twist on its original purpose.

Pinley

Pinley, not far away, presents a much more domestic and agricultural picture than Wroxall. It is a farm set amid fields,

27 *Wroxall Priory church.*

28   Probable prioress's house at Pinley Priory, late 15th-century, with the nuns' church rebuilt as a barn on the left.

the main house timber-framed and dated by Pevsner to about 1500, containing its original hall, chamber and kitchen with a spacious porch, which all suggest this could well have been the prioress's house. It is set at right angles to the west end of the church or rather what remains of the church, for apart from the west wall with its perpendicular doorway and the outline of a large window above, only a part of the north wall and the walls of the south transept remain, incorporated into a later farm building. If allowed to visit the site, a skilled eye could probably detect much more of Pinley's medieval priory.

Bristol

For the historian, the Bristol house of Augustinian canonesses has one great distinction among the Worcester nunneries: in the year 2000, the site underwent a thorough archaeological investigation. Inevitably post-medieval buildings prevented the whole site being studied, yet some useful results were achieved. Very likely the *King David Inn* stood on the site of the nuns' church and the tower and steeple of the church mentioned in 1554 were probably in the angle of St Michael's Hill and Upper Maudlin Street. To the north-west of the church the archaeologists found the lower courses of a medieval stone wall dating to the 12th or 13th century and thought to be one wall of the nuns' cloister. Not far from this discovery the excavation unearthed a number of skeletons, which were variously incomplete. These must point to the site of the monastic cemetery, customarily situated to the north of the church, in the same position as the other known burial ground at Whiston. Where the bones could be analysed, despite much being missing, they proved to be the remains of both men and women and ranged from pre-adult to elderly. Evidence of osteo-arthritis and anaemia were found, as well as other defects such as tooth decay and dental abscesses and long-term infections.[11] It may seem surprising to find male burials within the nuns' cemetery but this was not uncommon; they could well be those of the nuns' male servants. After all, of the two remaining servants at the Dissolution one was a man, or they could be the bones of the convent chaplain or of a favoured townsman whose family would pay the community a fee for his burial among them. Another parallel with Whiston nunnery is in the positioning of the church, in that both churches were built with their west end close to the public road running along the perimeter of the site. This would allow local people to enter the nave that they

Reproduced by permission of the Reference Library, Bristol Central Library.

29 King David Inn, *Bristol by Samuel Loxton c.1900. It was built in the early 18th century in the angle of St Michael's Hill and Upper Maudlin Street where the priory of St Mary Magdalen once stood. It probably incorporated elements of the monastic buildings.*

Reproduced by permission of the Reference Library, Bristol Central Library.

30   King David Inn, *Bristol by Samuel Loxton c.1900.*

might attend the nuns' services, as was customary, but with minimum intrusion into the monastic enclosure. Today there is no sign of the canonesses nunnery; it is buried beneath the spreading buildings of the Bristol Royal Infirmary.

Epilogue

The slight traces of the Worcester nunneries today do not do justice to the part they played in their local medieval world. Due to the nuns' limited resources, the restrictions imposed by their calling and because their contemporaries had low expectations of women as influential in society, they could never contribute as much as their male counterparts to the world around them. Nevertheless, holy women were not unimportant. Although Worcester did not own luminaries such as Hilda of Whitby or Julian of Norwich, in their 400 years of history the Worcester nunneries must have nurtured many noteworthy women, including prioresses who were confident leaders and managers and influential beyond the convent walls. The demands and expectations of their role could allow some to develop into women highly respected in their wider communities and in the church circles in which they moved. To a lesser degree the same was true of nuns with major posts within the convent, the obedientaries. For all these women, despite the stresses of authority, the monastery would provide a fulfilling life, developing character and talent in a way seldom open to their sisters in the world.

The nuns were enclosed from the world, yet they could not avoid being a part of it. When Benedict first set up a house for his sister, Scholastica, he hoped that this nunnery and all subsequent houses would be places set entirely apart but this proved an impossible concept. Inevitably all monasteries, male as well as female, became bound up in many ways with the society around them. One inevitable bond was their involvement in the local economy. To sustain their households the nuns had estates with urban properties as well as rural granges, farms and manors. All these holdings and lands meant dealing with tenants far and wide and taking part in the buying and selling of neighbourhood markets and in trade. Agents might do much of this for them but the nunneries remained an integral part of the local economy, dependent on rents and the profits of trade and farming for the well-being of the house. As lords of the manor – we only have surviving rolls for Westwood – the prioresses or their steward would not only have to manage the manor fields, pasture and meadow but also collect dues and taxes and dispense justice for quarrelling tenants.

The nuns no doubt benefited from the labour and offerings of their villeins and freemen but, as feudal overlords, they had to give in return. This was the whole point of the feudal system – everyone had their duties as well as their dues. On the nuns' manors the people could expect protection and care as far as was possible in return for the dues and offerings that they owed. The nuns could not give armed protection as other feudal lords might but instead they could give charity to the those in need. Charity and hospitality were sacred duties demanded by their Rule and all religious houses had to fulfil them. Any spare food or clothing would be passed on to the poor, and any who came to their gate must be welcomed as the Lord Christ himself. As the largest of the six nunneries, Westwood may have had a small guesthouse but there is no specific mention of such in any of the nunneries. No doubt important guests, such as the visiting bishop or a benefactor, would be put up in the prioress's lodging, while the ordinary travellers or even vagrants would find rest in an outbuilding or, at Westwood, perhaps in the habit. The guest mistress and the almoner, who could be one and the same person, might work alongside the infirmarian. She too would be dealing with the needy, hoping to bring some relief to the sick or injured with herbal skills and remedies passed down from one infirmarian to another.

All this charity was lost at the Dissolution. Poor men and women would have to look elsewhere for food and clothing, travellers whether rich or poor must use the hedgerow or the common inns rather than the monastery's sheltering walls, the sick could no longer come for remedy and, where once local parishioners had worshipped in the monastic church, now they must find another spiritual home. No evidence remains of the Worcester nuns' creative skills but probably in their time their communities included accomplished needlewomen who would sew and embroider elaborate vestments and altar furnishings. Others may have worked on copying texts with accompanying illumination. If these existed, they have now gone, another loss. Because any formal education was largely confined to boys, the nunneries had no equivalent of the male monastic schools. They did however encourage some learning and some had libraries of precious books such as at Nuneaton; again nothing has yet been identified for the Worcester female houses.

The destruction of the monasteries not only ended material benefits to the poor but also brought intellectual and spiritual loss. At their best, religious houses were places of learning and music, art and architecture as well as centres of Christianity. They were places of order and otherworldliness in sharp contrast to the squalor and uncertainty of much of medieval life. The monks and nuns were always there, following the pattern of life and worship as they had done before their neighbours were born and as they would do long after they had gone. They gave an unchanging continuity to society. But perhaps because they did not change life moved on beyond them. With the cataclysm of the Black Death and its long-ranging results, the growth of an urban society and the new ideas of the Renaissance and the Protestant reformers, monastic life lost its appeal and despite some late invigoration, came to appear old-fashioned and jaded. Some monasteries, as is too well known, became slack in spiritual discipline, with monks or nuns abandoning most of the Rule. Some of them, rather than withdrawing from the world, became all too much a part of it. The life of enclosure and poverty was often lost and the vow of celibacy ignored. Yet the loss of the monasteries brought by the Dissolution remains incalculable. They represented a spiritual ideal. Standing in the landscape, in the town or countryside, or in the wild desolate places, they reminded the world of those who had given up everything for Christ. The monks and nuns were those who had put aside family, possessions and their own wills for lives of work, worship and prayer. Monasteries were to be the spiritual powerhouses of society, out on the frontier battling with evil, constantly bringing the world's needs to God. Even if they often failed in their aspiration, the very existence of the abbeys and priories, of the hermitages and anchorholds, pointed society away from the material world to the timeless world of the spirit. In this great religious movement, the nunneries of the medieval Worcester diocese played their part and, although their communities were often far from perfect, they still remained exemplars of the sacrificial life for Christ, a striving for an ideal lived within the world, yet far removed from it.

Notes

I Holy Women of Worcestershire

1. Finberg, H.P.R., *The Early Charters of the West Midlands* (1961), p.135.
2. Hearne, T. (ed.), *Hemingi chartularium ecclesiae Wigorniensis. e codice MS penes Richardum Graves, etc.* (1723), p.464.
3. Dugdale, *Monasticon Anglicanum*, vol. 2, p.4.
4. William of Malmesbury, *The Life of St Wulstan*, trans. Peile, J.H.F. (1934), p.10.
5. Hockaday Abstracts, no. 432.
6. Calendar of Patent Rolls (1256), 49.
7. Close Rolls (1264-8), 7.
8. Whitehead, D., *Book of Worcester*, p.74.
9. Cotton MS D XV quoted by Elkins, S.E. in *Holy Women of Twelfth Century England*, pp.151-2.
10. Journal of Prior More (1521) (WHS), 136.
11. Journal of Prior More (1531) (WHS), 322.
12. Letters & Papers of Henry VIII XIII(ii), 49.
13. Register of Bishop Thomas Hemenhale, f12(d).
14. Register of Bishop Bransford (WHS), 137, no. 817.

II Founding

1. Kerr, B., *Religious Life for Women c1100-c1350* (1999), p.77.
2. Calendar of Patent Rolls (1476-89), 69.
3. Darlington, R.R. (ed.), Cartulary of Worcester Cathedral (WHS) vol. 38 (1968), 88, no. 162.
4. Owen, A.E.B, (ed.), *Lindsey Marsh. Select Documents* (1996), p.62.
5. Dugdale, *Monasticon*, vol. 6(2) 1006, Charter 15.
6. Cartulary of Worcester Cathedral, 88.
7. Register of Bishop Giffard (WHS), 8.
8. Pipe Rolls (1155-6), 62.
9. Papal Register, vol. 5, 405.
10. *VCH Worcestershire*, vol. 2, pp.156-7.
11. Calendar of Patent Rolls (1225-32), 167.
12. Close Rolls (1237-42), 310.

13. Valor Ecclesiasticus (1535), Cookhill Priory.
14. *VCH Warwickshire*, vol. 2, p.82.
15. Dugdale, *Monasticon*, IV, p.113.
16. Luard, H.R., (ed.), *Annales Monastici*, Rolls Series, vol. 4, p.443.
17. Close Rolls (1237-42), 274.
18. Liberate Rolls (1240-5), 30.
19. Liberate Rolls (1245-51), 6.
20. Close Rolls (1237-42), 310.
21. Close Rolls (1242-7), 333.
22. Thompson, S., 'The Problem of Cistercian Nuns' in Baker, D. (ed.), *Medieval Women* (1978).
23. *VCH of Warwickshire*, vol. 2, p.71.
24. Ibid.
25. Ibid.
26. Atkyns, R., *The Ancient and Present State of Gloucestershire* (1712), quoted in Dugdale, *Monasticon*, vol. 4, pp.589-90.
27. Calendar of Liberate Rolls (1245-51), 57.
28. Calendar of Liberate Rolls (1240-5), 37.
29. Register of Bishop Maidstone ,f29, HWRO BA 2648/1, iv.

III Cash and Kind

1. *VCH Warwickshire*, vol. 3, p.154.
2. Register of Bishop Giffard (WHS), 388.
3. Sede Vacante Register (WHS), 112.
4. Calendar of Patent Rolls (1297-1301), 595.
5. Calender of Patent Rolls (1334-8), 47, 185.
6. Worcester Liber Albus ff139, WCL, 140.
7. Calendar of Patent Rolls (1405-08), 260.
8. Original Charters of Worcester Cathedral no. 103, p.69.
9. Valor Ecclesiasticus, vol. 3, Whiston.
10. Valor Ecclesiaticus vol. 3, Cookhill.
11. Register of Bishop Cobham (WHS), 47.
12. Register of Bishop Giffard (WHS), 116, 267.
13. Register of Bishop Orleton (WHS), 66.
14. Calendar of Close Rolls (1333-7), 694.

15. Register of Bishop Clifford, f70, WRO BA 2648/5a.
16. Calendar of Close Rolls (1349-54), 621; (1354-60),186.
17. *VCH Warwickshire*, vol. 2, p.82.
18. Calendar of Patent Rolls (1292-1301), 616.
19. Wheler Galton, E.R., 'History of the Priory of Pinley', Warwick RO CR 2310 (*c*.1930).
20. Register of Bishop Polton, f12b, WRO BA2648/5b.
21. Russell, J.C., 'The Clerical Population of Medieval England' in *Traditio* (1949), p.177.
22. Calendar of Patent Rolls (1385-9), 27.
23. Power, E., *Medieval English Nunneries* (1922), p.213.
24. National Archives SCC6/Hen 8/4042.
25. Power, E., *Medieval English Nunneries* (1922), p.198.
26. *VCH Lincolnshire*, vol. 2, 131.
27. Kerr, B., *Religious Life for Women* (1999), p.154.
28. Sede Vacante Register (WHS), 120.
29. Register of Bishop Giffard (WHS), 231.
30. Miller, E. and Hatcher, J., *Medieval England: Rural Society and Economic Change* (1978), p.60.
31. Creighton, J., *History of Epidemics in Britain from AD 644 to the Present Time*, vol.1, p.19.
32. Calendar of Patent Rolls (1266-72), 498.
33. Hampton Papers, 306.
34. Calendar of Patent Rolls (1272-81), 232.
35. Hampton Papers, 53; 86.
36. Calendar of Patent Rolls (1343-6), 383.
37. Calender of Patent Rolls (1313-17), 499.
38. Kerr, B., *Religious Life for Women*, p.188.
39. Hampton Papers, 313, WRO.
40. Hampton Papers, 309, WRO.
41. Dugdale, *Monasticon*, vol. 6(2), charter 37, 1009.
42. Dugdale, *Monasticon*, vol. 6(2), charters 36,1009; 28,1008.
43. Kerr, B., *Religious Life for Women*, p.220.
44. Hampton Papers, 319, WRO.
45. Dugdale, *Monasticon*, charters 28, 1008; 42, 1010.
46. Hampton Papers, 308, WRO.
47. Kerr, B., *Religious Life for Women*, p.220.
48. Tillotson, J.H., 'Marrick Priory', Borthwick Paper, 75 (1989), 10, 30.
49. Hampton Papers, 309, WRO.
50. Hampton Papers, 308, 316, WRO.
51. Calendar of Patent Rolls (1399-1401), 374; (1405-08), 315.
52. Kerr, B., *Religious Life for Women*, p.157.

IV Life in the Nunnery

1. Kerr, B., *Religious Life for Women*, p.102.
2. Register of Bishop Hemenale, f12, WRO BA648/2.
3. Worcester Liber Albus, f282.
4. Worcester Liber Albus, f425.
5. Register of Bishop Polton, f14, WRO BA2648/5b.
6. Register of Bishop Alcock, f153, WRO BA.
7. *VCH Warwickshire*, vol. 2, p.82.
8. Graham, R., 'The Metropolitical Visitation of the Diocese of Worcester by Archbishop Winchelsey' in *English Ecclesiastical Studies*, p.66.
9. Sede Vacante Register (WHS), 112.
10. Register of Bishop Reynolds (WHS), 29.
11. Register of Bishop Giffard (WHS), 231.
12. Kerr, B., *Religious Life for Women*, p.161.
13. Register of Bishop Cobham (WHS), 162.
14. Calendar of Patent Rolls (1385-9), 207.
15. Power, E., *Medieval English Nunneries*, p.332.
16. Dobson, E.J., *The Origins of the Ancrene Wisse* (1976), pp.90-1.
17. Ibid., p.89.
18. Power, E., *Medieval English Nunneries*, p.304.
19. Register of Bishop Wittlesey, f7, WRO BA 2648/4(ii).

V Discipline and Authority

1. Calendar of Patent Rolls (1339-1401), 374.
2. Register of Bishop Allcock, f167, WRO BA 2648/4(ii).
3. Calendar of Patent Rolls (1292-1301), 616.
4. Register of Bishop Reynolds (WHS), 10.
5. Register of Bishop Hemenale, f12, WRO BA 2648 2b(iii).
6. Worcester Liber Albus, f90d.
7. Sede Vacante Register (WHS), 96.
8. Sede Vacante Register (WHS), 111-15.
9. Calendar of Close Rolls (1323-7), 426.
10. Register of Bishop Bransford (WHS), 60-1.
11. Ibid. 176, 428.
12. Register of Bishop Morgan, f6d, WRO BA2648/3.
13. Catalogue of the Medieval Muniments at Berkeley Castle, vol. 1 (2004), 556.
14. National Archives SC 1/34/128.
15. Nash, T., *History of Worcestershire*, vol. 2 (1781), p.354.
16. Registers of Bishop Giffard (WHS), 165, 284; of Bishop Bransford (WHS), 23; of Bishop Montacute (WHS), 279.
17. Registers of Bishop Montacute (WHS), 279; of Bishop Bransford (WHS), 23.
18. Sede Vacante Register (WHS), 273, 396.
19. Register of Bishop Giffard (WHS), 515.
20. Power, E., *Medieval English Nunneries*, p.382.
21. Sede Vacante Register (WHS) 278

22. Register of Bishop Montacute (WHS), 210.
23. Register of Bishop Giffard (WHS), 267.
24. Sede Vacante Register (WHS), 277-8.
25. Register of Bishop Thoresby, f11, WRO BA 2648/3(ii).
26. Register of Bishop Cobham (WHS), 161-3.
27. Register of Bishop Bransford (WHS), 60-1.
28. Langland, W., *The Vision of Piers the Plowman*, Skeat, Walter (ed.) (1869), Passus X, l94.
29. Sede Vacante Register (WHS), 276-8.
30. Register of Bishop Reynolds (WHS), 27.
31. Will Register, vol. 1, f25 (1470), WRO BA 3590/1.
32. www.oginet.com/chronicles/wwm1455.htm.

VI   The End

1. Preamble to the Act for the Dissolution of the Lesser Monasteries (1536).
2. *VCH Lincolnshire*, vol. 2, p.154.
3. *VCH Warwickshire*, vol. 2, p.72, p.83.
4. *VCH Gloucestershire*, vol. 2, p.93.
5. *VCH Worcestershire*, vol. 2, p.156 (Whiston); Letters and Papers of Henry VIII vol. XIII(i), p.576 (Westwood); *VCH Warwickshire*, vol. 2, p.72 (Wroxall); Ibid., p.83 (Pinley).
6. *VCH Gloucestershire*, vol. 2, p.93.
7. National Archives SC6 Henry VIII, 4042.
8. Letters and Papers Henry VIII, vol. XVII, 704.
9. Ibid., vol. XI, 567.
10. Ibid., vol. XV, 35.
11. Bettey, J.H., *The Suppression of the Monasteries in the West Country* (1989), 126.
12. Oliva, M., 'Unsafe Passage' in Greatrex, J. (ed.), *The Vocation of Service to God and Neighbour* (1998).
13. Baskerville, G., *English Monks and the Suppression of the Monasteries* (1937), p.217.
14. Ibid., p.223.
15. Bettey, J.H., *Suppression*, p.111.
16. *VCH Warwickshire*, vol. 2, p.83.
17. Bettey, J.H., *Suppression*, pp.36-7.
18. *VCH Warwickshire*, vol. 2, p.83 (Pinley); ibid., p.72 (Wroxall); *VCH Gloucestershire*, vol. 2, p.93 (Bristol).
19. National Archives SC6 Henry VIII, 4042.

20. Register of Sede Vacante (WHS), 307.
21. Worcester Liber Albus f424, 425, WCL.
22. Letters and Papers of Henry VIII, vol. IX, p.155.
23. Letters and Papers of Henry VIII, vol. X, p.155.
24. Ibid., vol. XI, p.120.
25. Ibid., vol. XX(ii), p.225.
26. Longman, T., 'Excavations on the Site of the Priory of St Mary Magdalen' in *Bristol and Avon Archaeology*, vol. 18 (2001), p.4.
27. Letters and Papers of Henry VIII, vol. IX, p.498.
28. *VCH Warwickshire*, vol. 2, p.83.
29. Wheler Galton, E.R., 'History of the Priory of Pinley, Warwick', RO CR 2310 (*c*.1930).
30. *VCH Warwickshire*, vol. 3, pp.150-1.
31. Letters and Papers of Henry VIII, vol. VIX(ii), p.472.
32. *VCH Warwickshire*, vol. 2, p.72.
33. Will Register, VI(2) no. 72(a) 196 WRO BA3590.
34. Ibid., no. 138, 155.
35. Leland, J., *Itinerary in England and Wales 1535-43*, Toulmin-Smith, L. (ed.), vol. V (1908), p.91.

VII   Remnants and Ruins

1. Habington, T., *A Survey of Worcestershire*, Amphlett, J. (ed.) (WHS) (1895), p.459.
2. Prattinton Collection, WRO BA10509 9899:9 (xii).
3. British Archaeological Association, 'Visit to Worcester 1848', Dunkin, A.J. (ed.) (1851).
4. Gwilliam, H.W., 'Old Worcester People and Places' (typescript, 1977), vol. 2, p.50.
5. WRO BA 372.
6. Six Masters Plans (1826), WRO BA 3617/1, 2.
7. Green, V., *History of Worcestershire*, vol. 1 (1796), p.241.
8. *VCH Worcestershire*, vol. 3, p.419.
9. Nash, T., *Survey of Worcestershire*, vol. 1, p.156.
10. *VCH Worcestershire*, vol. 3, p.420.
11. Longman, T., 'Excavations' in *Bristol and Avon Archaeology*, vol. 18 (2001), pp.3-29.

Bibliography

The following abbreviations are used:

TWAS *Transactions of the Worcester Archaeological Society*
WAS   Worcester Archaeological Society
WCL   Worcester Cathedral Library
WRO   Worcester Record Office
WHS   Worcester Historical Society

Primary Sources

Published Registers

Register of Bishop Giffard, Bund, J.W. (ed.), WHS 1902
Register of Bishop Ginsborough, Bund, J.W. (ed.), WHS 1907
Registrum Sede Vacante, Bund, J.W. (ed.), WHS 1897
Register of Bishop Orleton, Haines, R.M. (ed.), WHS 1979
Register of Bishop Montacute, Haines, R.M. (ed.),WHS 1996
Register of Bishop Bransford, Haines, R.M. (ed.), WHS 1966
Register of Bishop Wakefield, Marrett, W.P. (ed.), WHS 1972
Register of Bishop Cobham, Pearce, E.H. (ed.),WHS 1930
Register of Bishop Reynolds, Wilson, R.A. (ed.),WHS 1927

MSS Registers

Register of Bishop Alcock, WRO BA2648/7
Register of Bishop Carpenter, WRO BA2648/6
Register of Bishop Clifford, WRO BA2648/5a
Register of Bishop Hemenale, WRO BA2648/2
Register of Bishop Maidstone, WRO BA2648/1
Register of Bishop Morgan, WRO BA 2648/5
Register of Bishop Polton, WRO BA2648/5b
Register of Bishop Thoresby, WRO BA 2648/3
Register of Bishop Wittesley, WRO BA2648/4

Published

Almoner's Book of the Priory of Worcester, Harvey Booth, J. (ed.),WHS 1911
Annales Monastici, Luard, H.R. (ed.), Rolls Series 1864-9
Calendar of Close Rolls
Calendar of Liberate Rolls
Calendar of Papal Registers
Calendar of Patent Rolls
Cartulary of Worcester Cathedral Priory, Darlington, R. (ed.), London 1968
Evesham Chronicle, Macray, W.D. (ed.), Rolls Series 1863
Faculty Office Registers 1534-1549, Chambers, D.S. (ed.), Oxford 1966
Journal of Prior More, WHS 1913
Inquisitions post Mortem for the County of Worcestershire, Bund, J.W. Willis (ed.), WHS 1894
Letters and Papers of Henry VIII
Liber Pensionum of the Priory of Worcester, Price, C. (ed.), WHS 1925
Original Charters relating to the City of Worcester, Harvey Bloom, J. (ed.), WHS 1909
Pipe Roll Society
Red Book of Worcester, Hollings, M. (ed.), WHS 1902
Worcester Liber Albus (in part), WHS
Worcester Will Register, Fry, E.A. (ed.), WHS WRO BA3590/1

MSS

Catalogue of Muniments of Worcester Cathedral, Benedikz, R.S., Brock, S.L. and Pick, G.M.B. (ed.), 1981, WCL
Hampton Papers, Worcester Record Office
Hockaday Abstracts, Gloucestershire Record Office
Hodgkinson Papers, WRO BA 2251
Pakington Papers, WRO BA3835
Palfrey Collection of Engravings and Watercolours, WRO 3678
Prattinton Collection, WRO BA 385, BA 10509
Six Masters Survey Book, WRO BA3617/6
Worcester Liber Albus, WCL

Secondary Sources

Anderson, B.S. and Zinsser, J.P., *A History of their own: Women in Europe from Prehistory to Present* (1988)
Baker, D. (ed.), *Medieval Women* (1978)
Barnard, E.A.B.,'The Pakingtons of Westwood', *TWAS*, vol.XIII (1936)
Baskerville, G., *English Monks and the Suppression of the Monasteries* (1937)
Bettey, J.H., *The Suppression of the Monasteries in the West Country* (1989)

Bradbrook, W., *History of the Parish of Inkberrow and Local Government*, WAS (1973)

Burton, J., 'Yorkshire Nunneries', *Borthwick Papers*, no. 56 (1979)

Burton, J., *Monastic and Religious Orders in Britain* (1994)

Carver, M.O.H., *Medieval Worcester*, WAS 1980

Chibnall, M., *The World of Orderic Vitalis* 1994

Coldicott, D., *Hampshire Nunneries* (1989)

Coss, P., *The Lady in Medieval England 1000-1500* (1998)

Dobson, E.J., *The Origins of the Ancrene Wisse* (1976)

Driver, J.T., 'Knights of the Shire', *TWAS*, vol. 5 (1976)

Duffy, E., *The Stripping of the Altars* (1992)

Dugdale, W. and others, *Monasticon Anglicanum* (1823)

Dyer, A.J., *The City of Worcester in the Sixteenth Century* (1973)

Dyer, C., *Standards of Living in the Later Middle Ages* (1989)

Elkins, S.K., *Holy Women of the Twelfth Century* (1988)

Finberg, H.P.R., *The Early Charters of the West Midlands* (1961)

Follett, E.V., *The History of Worcester Royal Grammar School* (1951)

Gies, F. and J., *Women in the Middle Ages* (1980)

Gilchrist, R. and Oliva, M., *Religious Women in Medieval East Anglia* (1993)

Graham, R., 'The Metropolitical Visitation of the Diocese of Worcester by Archbishop Winchelsey in 1301', *English Ecclesiastical Studies* (1921)

Green, V., *History of Worcester* (1796)

Habington, T., *Survey of Worcestershire*, Amphlett, J. (ed.) (1895-9)

Haines, R.M., *The Administration of the Diocese of Worcester in the First Half of the Fourteenth century* (1965)

Harrison, M.J., *The Nunnery of Nun Appleton*, Borthwick Paper no.98 (2001)

Harvey, B., *Living and Dying in England 1100-1540: The Monastic Experience*, (1993)

Heath, P., *Church and Realm 1272-1461* (1988)

Hillaby, J., 'St Oswald, the Revival of Monasticism and the Veneration of the Saints in the Late Anglo Saxon and Norman Diocese of Worcester', *TWAS*, vol.16 (1998)

Hunt, R. and Jackson, R., *More About the Parish of Inkberrow* (1976)

Hurst, J.D., *Savouring the Past: The Droitwich Salt Industry* (1992)

Keevil, G., Aston, M. and Hall, T. (eds), *Monastic Archaeology* (2001)

Kerr, B., *Religious Life for Women 1100-1350* (1999)

Kingsbury, J.G., 'Nunnery and Perry Woods', *TWAS*, vol. 9 (1984)

Knowles, D., *Religious Orders in England*, vol.2 (1971)

Knowles, D. and Hadcock, R., *Medieval Religious Houses in England and Wales* (1971)

Knowles, D., Brooke, C.N.L. and London, V., *Heads of Religious Houses in England and Wales 940-1216* (1972)

Labarge, M. Wade, *Women in Medieval Life: A Small Sound of the Trumpet* (1986)

Langland, W., *The Vision of Piers the Plowman*, ed. Skeat, W.W. (1869)

Lawrence, C.H., *Medieval Monasticism* (1997)

Lees, E., 'The History of the Convent of the White Ladies of Worcester', *TWAS*, vol.VIII (1865-6)

Leland, J., *Itinerary 1535-1543*, ed. Toulmin Smith, L. (1964)

Logan, F.D., *Runaway Religious in Medieval England 1240-1540* (1996)

Logan, F.D., 'Departure from the Religious Life during the Royal Visitation of the Monasteries', in Clark, J. (ed.), *The Religious Orders in Pre- Reformation England* (2002)

Longman, T., 'Excavations on the Site of the Priory of St Mary Magdalen, Upper Maudlin St, Bristol, 2000', in *Bristol and Avon Archaeology*, vol.18 (2002)

Makowski, E., *Canon Law and Cloistered Women: Periculoso and its Commentators 1298-1545* (1997)

Mason, E., 'Life Influence', in Brookes, N. and Cubitt, C. (eds), *St Oswald of Worcester* (1996)

Miller, E., and Hatcher, J., *Medieval England: Rural Society and Economic Change 1086-1348* (1978)

Moorhouse, G., *The Pilgrimage of Grace* (2002)

Moran, J.A.H., 'Clerical Recruitment in the Diocese of York 1360-1530', in *Journal of Ecclesiastical History*, vol.34 (1983)

Mould, A., *The English Chorister* (2006)

Nash, T., *Collections for the History of Worcestershire* (1781)

Neale, F., 'William Worcester: Bristol Churches in 1480' in Bettey, J. (ed.), *Historic Churches and Church Life in Bristol* (2001)

Oliva, M., 'Unsafe Passage', in Greatrex, J. (ed.), *The Vocation of Service to God and Neighbour* (1998)

Owen, D.M., 'Church and Society', in *Medieval Lincolnshire* (1971)

Owen, A.E.B., *The Medieval Lindsey Marsh. Select Documents*, Lincoln Record Society (1996)

Parry, Y., 'Devoted Disciples of Christ: Early Religious Life at Amesbury', in *Journal of Historical Research*, vol.67 (1994)

Pevsner, N., *Warwickshire* (1996)

Platt, C., *Medieval England* (1978)

Platt, C., *Abbeys and Priories of Medieval England* (1984)

Platt, C., *King Death* (1996)

Power, E., *Medieval English Nunneries* (1922)

Russell, J.C., 'The Clerical Population of Medieval England', in *Traditio* (1949)

Ryland, J.W., *Records of Wroxall Abbey* (1902)

Swanson, R.N., 'Titles to Orders in Medieval English Episcopal Registers', in Mayr-Harting, H. and Moore, R.I. (eds), *Studies in Medieval History* (1985)

Swanson, R.N., *Religion and Devotion in Europe 1215-1515* (1997)

Tanner, T., *Notitia Monastica* (1744)

Taylor, C.S., 'The Religious Houses of Bristol', *Transactions of the Bristol and Gloucester Archaeological Society* (1906)

Thomas, W., *A Survey of the Cathedral Church of Worcester* (1736)

Thompson, J.A.F., 'Piety and Charity in late Medieval London', *Journal of Ecclesiastical History*, vol.16 (1965)

Thompson, S., 'The Problem of the Cistercian Nuns', in Baker, D. (ed.), *Medieval Women* (1978)

Thompson, S., *Women Religious: The Founding of the English Nunneries after the Norman Conquest* (1991)

Tillotson, J.H., *Marrick Priory*, Borthwick Paper no.75 (1989)

Titow, J.Z., *English Rural Society* (1969)

Turner, C.M. (ed.), *Early Worcester Manuscripts* (1916)

Veasey, E.A., *From Eaton to Nuneaton*

Victoria History of the Counties of England: Gloucestershire, Lincolnshire, Warwickshire, Worcestershire

Whitehead, D., *The Book of Worcester* (1976)

Whitehouse, D.B., 'Post-medieval Pottery from Worcestershire', *TWAS*, vol. XXXIX (1962)

William of Malmesbury, *The Life of St Wulstan*, trans. Peile, J.H.F. (1934)

Woodward, C.W.O., *The Dissolution of the Monasteries* (1966)

Unpublished

Gwillam, H.W., 'Old Worcester People and Places', vol.2 (1977)

Hodgkinson, H.R., 'St Mary's Priory Westwood', WRO

Pakington, H. and R., 'The Pakingtons of Westwood' (1975)

Wheler Galton, E.R., 'History of the Priory of Pinley', Warwick RO (*c.*1930)

Index